'TWIXT LONDON AND BRISTOL

Michael Hale

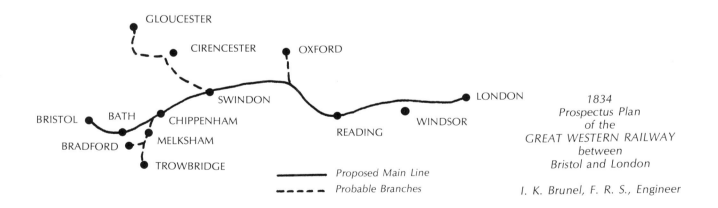

1834
Prospectus Plan
of the
GREAT WESTERN RAILWAY
between
Bristol and London

I. K. Brunel, F. R. S., Engineer

Oxford Publishing Company

Typesetting by:
Aquarius Typesetting Services, New Milton, Hants.

Printed in Great Britain by:
Biddles Ltd., Guildford, Surrey.

Published by:
Oxford Publishing Co.
Link House
West Street
POOLE, Dorset

Introduction

At the dawn of the locomotive-worked railway age, it was only to be expected that proposals should be put forward for such a link between London and the important port of Bristol. After several false starts, a committee representing the commercial and civic interests of Bristol was set up to look into the details. On 7th March 1833, an engineer was appointed to carry out a survey of the route; a man only twenty seven years of age, but not unknown in the city — Isambard Kingdom Brunel.

Support was canvassed and a similar committee was formed in London. The first joint meeting of the two committees was held on 19th August 1833, when the title of Great Western Railway was adopted. After much discussion and some modification, their proposals were eventually approved by both Houses of Parliament and the Great Western Railway Bill received the Royal Assent on 31st August 1835. That date is taken to be the birth of the GWR, and its 150th Anniversary will be commemorated in various ways during 1985.

The Company was empowered to build a railway 'commencing at or near a certain Field called Temple Mead . . . in the City of Bristol . . . passing through specified Parishes in the Counties of Gloucester, Somerset, Wilts, Berks, Oxford, Bucks and Middlesex . . . and terminating by a Junction with the London & Birmingham Railway in a certain Field . . . in the Parish of Hammersmith . . . Also a branch railway from near Thingley Farm, in the Parish of Corsham, to a Field near the Gas Works in the part of the Parish of Trowbridge called Islington, with another branch thereout from the south-western extremity of the Village of Holt in the Parish of Bradford, to the farmyard of Kingston Farm adjoining the Town of Bradford.' The proposed junction with the L&BR was abandoned, and in the fol-lowing year another Act authorised an extension of the line from Acton to 'a certain space of ground adjoining the Basin of the Paddington Canal in the Parish of Paddington.'

Brunel constructed the railway to the gauge of 7ft. 0¼in., rather than to the narrow gauge of 4ft. 8½in. which quickly became standard. Whatever technical merit the broad gauge might have had, and the subject aroused heated arguments, it served only to isolate the GWR and its associated companies from those in the rest of the country. It was gradually done away with, its use ceasing completely in 1892.

The Railways Act of 1921 brought a number of smaller railways into GWR ownership, but the Company continued under its own name, by then the oldest of all. That was ended by the Act of Nationalisation, effective from 1st January 1948, and it became evident that GWR practices would have little part to play in the new order. Even so, GWR locomotives, rolling stock, stations and other structures continued in use for over a quarter of a century, as can be seen in this photographic survey of the main line and its branches.

The general history of the Company and its locomotives has been well documented, and biographies of its senior officers written. This volume is gratefully dedicated to ordinary men and women whose names do not appear in the history books; those whose tacit co-operation enabled many of the photographs to be taken; those who, in former days, would have been called servants of the Company, and proud to be so; those who, after nationalisation, in different ways and at different levels of employment, endeavoured to uphold the best traditions of the Great Western Railway.

Michael Hale
Dudley
September 1984

Acknowledgements

The historical details given in this book were obtained from various sources, amongst which, publications by the following organisations and individuals have been particularly helpful: The Great Western Railway and its foremost historian, E. T. MacDermot, British Railways (Western Region), Branch Line Society, Railway Correspondence & Travel Society, Signalling Record Society, Stephenson Locomotive Society, G. Body, C. R. Clinker, R. A. Cooke, E. Lyons, C. G. Maggs, E. R. Mountford and T. B. Peacock

Plate 1

On 28th November 1837, a 2-2-2 tender locomotive named *North Star* was delivered to the Great Western Railway at Maidenhead. It was transported by river barge as rails had not then reached that point. Robert Stephenson & Co. of Newcastle had built the locomotive for the 5ft. 6in. gauge New Orleans Railway, but it was left on their hands, so they converted it to 7ft. gauge. *North Star* worked the first passenger train on the GWR, a Directors' special from Hayes to the original Maidenhead Station, on 31st May 1838. In a modified form, the locomotive was preserved at Swindon Works until 1906, when the space which it occupied was required for other purposes. After attempts to find another home for it had failed, most regrettably, it was cut up. For the 1925 Railway Centenary celebrations, a full size replica of the as-built locomotive was constructed. Subsequently, it was displayed as shown, on a pedestal in the main erecting shop at Swindon Works. Also visible are driving wheels from another broad gauge engine, *Lord of the Isles*, which was also cut up in 1906. These items are now displayed in the GWR Museum at Swindon.

14th June 1953

London and Suburbs

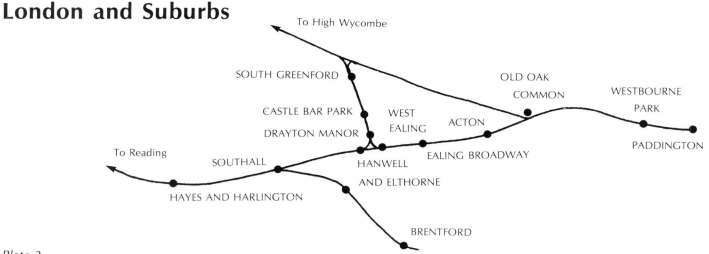

Plate 2

From 16th September 1957, the 7.45 train from Hereford to Paddington was named the 'Cathedrals Express'. The stock, which returned from Paddington at 4.45, was painted in the former GWR colours of chocolate and cream; a livery which was applied to several Western Region named trains at that time. Through carriages to and from Kidderminster were also included, and the number of intermediate stops must have caused some passengers to question the 'express' rating. Here, 4-6-0 No. 4088 *Dartmouth Castle*, from Worcester Shed, is seen bringing the train into Paddington, where vans stand alongside the parcels depot in the background. Seated on a luggage trolley, a boy with his notebook symbolises the many enthusiasts who have gathered at Paddington to watch Great Western engines.

4th March 1959

Facilities provided at Paddington for the opening day, Monday 4th June 1838, were rather primitive and were soon replaced by a proper station. This proved to be inadequate for the developing traffic and a larger station was opened during 1854, to the east of the Bishop's Road bridge. It was designed by I. K. Brunel in conjunction with Sir Matthew Digby Wyatt, a noted architect. In the course of improvements carried out in later years, efforts have been made to retain the features associated with the great engineer.

Plate 3
A station at Westbourne Park was opened in 1871. When photographed, it had four platform faces, but now it consists of an island platform serving only the relief lines. For many years there was an important locomotive depot here, with separate sheds for broad and narrow gauge engines. The greater part of it lay on the far side of the road bridge, and it was closed in 1906 when more spacious accommodation was brought into use at Old Oak Common.

5th August 1962

The following were noted during a visit to Old Oak Common on 29th April 1951: Nos. 1000 *County of Middlesex*, 1500, 1503, 1504, 1505, 2208, 2276, 2282, 2800, 2825, 2826, 2854, 2858, 2860, 2868, 2895, 3648, 3688, 3715, 3754, 3803, 3805, 3813, 3841, 3852, 3853, 4007 *Swallowfield Park*, 4031 *Queen Mary*, 4037 *The South Wales Borderers*, 4053 *Princess Alexandra*, 4095 *Harlech Castle*, 4615, 4644, 4698, 4699, 4702, 4705, 4948 *Northwick Hall*, 4964 *Rodwell Hall*, 4998 *Eyton Hall*, 5012 *Berry Pomeroy Castle*, 5039 *Rhuddlan Castle*, 5043 *Earl of Mount Edgcumbe*, 5052 *Earl of Radnor*, 5055 *Earl of Eldon*, 5061 *Earl of Birkenhead*, 5064 *Bishop's Castle*, 5066 *Wardour Castle*, 5076 *Gladiator*, 5087 *Tintern Abbey*, 5095 *Barbury Castle*, 5764, 5932 *Hayden Hall*, 5936 *Oakley Hall*, 5937 *Stanford Hall*, 5941 *Campion Hall*, 5942 *Doldowlod Hall*, 5980 *Dingley Hall*, 5989 *Cransley Hall*, 5991 *Gresham Hall*, 6001 *King Edward VII*, 6003 *King George IV*, 6006 *King George I*, 6007 *King William III*, 6011 *King James I*, 6012 *King Edward VI*, 6015 *King Richard III*, 6019 *King Henry V*, 6028 *King George VI*, 6106, 6113, 6119, 6120, 6121, 6135, 6136, 6141, 6155, 6164, 6168, 6354, 6874 *Haughton Grange*, 6959 *Peatling Hall*, 6974 *Bryngwyn Hall*, 7001 *Sir James Milne*, 7004 *Eastnor Castle*, 7013 *Bristol Castle*, 7024 *Powis Castle*, 7025 *Sudeley Castle*, 7027 *Thornbury Castle*, 7030 *Cranbrook Castle*, 7032 *Denbigh Castle*, 7791, 7903 *Foremarke Hall*, 8707, 8750, 8751, 8757, 8759, 8760, 8761, 8762, 8764, 8765, 8767, 8769, 8770, 8771, 8772, 8773, 9301, 9302, 9305, 9309, 9403, 9405, 9406, 9418, 9419, 9420, 9659, 9700, 9701, 9702, 9705, 9706, 9708, 9709, 9710, 9751, 9754, 9758, 9784, diesel-electric shunters Nos. 15101, 15105 and gas turbine No. 18000.

Plate 4 (above)
The locomotive depot at Old Oak Common was the largest on the GWR system, with an allocation of over 200 engines for all types of duty. It comprised four roundhouses under one roof, and a repair shop with 12 bays. It was coded PDN by the GWR, although sometimes OOC was seen, or 81A by BR, and it was closed to steam in March 1965. Seen inside one of the roundhouses is 0-6-0PT No. 8763, lined out in red, cream and grey. In BR days, most members of the class were painted unlined black, but a few were given the mixed traffic livery, and used on empty stock workings in and out of Paddington.

4th October 1953

Plate 6 (right)
A station was opened at Ealing in December 1839 and, in later years, as Ealing Broadway it became an interchange point between GWR suburban services and London Transport. In 1965, a new station was opened as part of a development scheme which included an office block and shopping centre.

21st August 1960

Plate 5 (below left)
The name of Acton was well-known on the GWR for its large marshalling yard, but here is the passenger station, which opened in 1868 and which was designated Acton (Main Line) from 26th September 1949.

5th August 1962

Plate 7 (below)
West Ealing Station was opened in 1871 as Castle Hill, and the name was changed in 1899. Again, there were four platforms at the time of the photograph, but only two faces now remain in use. As it was the last station before the Greenford branch diverged, the nameboard proclaimed it to be the junction for that line.

5th August 1962

The Greenford Branch

Plate 8
The Greenford branch was opened on 3rd June 1903, and a circular service from Paddington operated for three weeks in connection with the Royal Agricultural Show at Park Royal. The triangular junction with the main line can be seen when looking past the platforms of Drayton Green Halt, which were opened on 1st March 1905.

5th August 1962

Plate 9
A regular passenger service commenced on 1st May 1904, on which date Castle Bar Park Halt was opened, although the platforms shown date from 1960. Details of the services are too complicated to be given here, and varied over the years. At first they were operated by steam railmotors, and later by auto-trains, but steam working ceased in August 1958.

6th August 1962

Plate 10
South Greenford Halt was opened on 20th September 1926. The suffix 'Halt' was dropped from 5th May 1969, but the three stopping places remain in use, served by diesel rail-cars running between Ealing Broadway and Greenford. Part of the line is now covered by a tunnel, to allow housing development to spread over it.

5th August 1962

Plate 11
The original Hanwell Station was planned for the opening of the GWR, but it was not ready until December 1838. This view shows the relief line platforms, with the 'up' loop and engineer's sidings in the Greenford branch triangle in the distance. Although the nameboard still reads 'Hanwell and Elthorne', the latter name was officially dropped in November 1959. The station was modernised in 1981.

5th August 1962

Southall

Plate 12
Southall Shed lay in the fork of the main line and the Brentford branch, which can be seen going off to the right. The original small shed here was opened in 1884, but the eight-road building shown dates from 1954, and once had an allocation of over 70 locomotives, plus a few diesel railcars. The depot was coded SHL (GWR) or 81C (BR), and closed to steam at the end of 1965.

5th August 1962

Plate 13 (above)
Speeding through Southall Station, 4-6-0 No. 7011 *Banbury Castle* heads the 1.35 express from Bristol, due in Paddington at 4.30. The first station here opened on 1st May 1839.

17th May 1959

Plate 14 (below)
Nos. 5415, 5727, 1443, 9406 and 3843 are shown at the rear of Southall Shed, the first three being stored out of use, but not yet withdrawn. Also noted during that visit were Nos. 1415, 1436, 1446, 1501, 2822, 2857, 2899, 3206, 3620, 3704, 3727, 3799, 3803, 3814, 3819, 4608, 4610, 4673, 4695, 5371, 5420, 5925 *Eastcote Hall*, 5983 *Henley Hall*, 6109, 6119, 6120, 6128, 6147, 6165, 6169, 6991 *Acton Burnell Hall*, 7730, 7731, 8750, 8752, 8758, 9409, 9417, 9710, 9789, 90313, 90485, 90579 and diesel railcars W27, W30 and W31.

12th August 1956

Plate 15
Here is another view from the footbridge at the east end of Southall Station, showing 4-6-0 No. 6004 *King George III* with the 4.15 express from Paddington to Plymouth, via Bristol. The goods shed and yard, seen on the left, closed from 2nd January 1967. The GWR Preservation Group has had a railway centre at Southall for several years, but the site is now threatened by redevelopment plans.

17th May 1959

Plate 16
The Brentford branch was built to link the GWR main line with a dock on the River Thames, and it opened for goods on 15th July 1859, with a passenger service from 1st May 1860. Traffic was worked by the GWR, although the railway was a nominally independent one until taken over in 1872. Broad gauge rails were removed in 1875. The derelict platforms of Brentford Station, seen here, with the Town Goods Depot in the distance, had lost their passenger service from 4th May 1942. The section down to the dock closed completely from 31st December 1964, and the Town Goods closed in 1970, leaving only private sidings.

6th August 1962

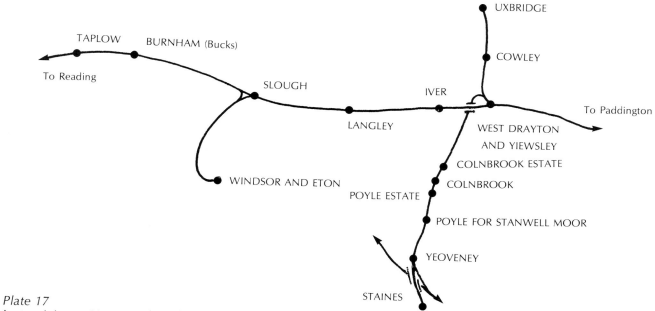

Plate 17

Just arriving at Hayes and Harlington, 2-6-2T No. 6150 is working the 4.33 semi-fast from Paddington to Reading. Hayes Station was opened in 1864, and the word 'Harlington' was added to the name in 1897. The buildings were modernised in 1962. A timber-creosoting depot was situated on the 'down' side for many years, but it closed in 1964. The goods yard closed from 2nd January 1967.

17th May 1959

Plate 18
This view of West Drayton Station, facing towards London, shows that the nameboard then read 'West Drayton & Yiewsley, Junction for Uxbridge & Staines', but both those branches have since closed. West Drayton is of some importance in GWR history, as it was not only the site of one of the original stations, but also the locomotive headquarters in early days. The first two engines to work on the railway, *Premier* and *Vulcan*, were given trials here after being delivered by sea and canal in 1837.

7th August 1962

To Uxbridge and Staines

A single line branch to Uxbridge was opened on 8th September 1856; it was converted to standard gauge in 1871 and doubled in 1880. The Staines branch was promoted by a nominally independent company, the Staines & West Drayton Railway, but it was worked by the GWR and formally absorbed in 1900. It was opened from a new station at West Drayton to Colnbrook on 9th August 1884, and through to Staines on 2nd November 1885.

Plate 19
To the west of the station, the Uxbridge branch diverges and then, after a quarter of a mile, the Staines branch bears away to curve south and pass under the main line. In 1960, a new signal box was commissioned in connection with a new layout for a coal concentration depot in the loop of the branch, but it had a life of only ten years. In this view, the old West box, the new branch box and the goods shed can be seen in the distance.

7th August 1962

Plates 20 & 21

The only intermediate station on the Uxbridge branch, at Cowley (above), was opened on 2nd October 1904. Uxbridge (Vine Street) Station (below), named thus when High Street Station was opened in 1907, originally had an overall roof, but it was modified in the 1930s, and this photograph shows its final run-down state. An engine shed, which closed in 1901, once stood on the right, and the goods yard was on the left. In the early 1950s, the branch saw about 30 trains each way daily, worked by an assortment of auto-trains, GWR railcars, and 61XX tank engines for the dozen or so through trains to Paddington. BR diesel units took over for the last few years, but the branch closed to passengers from 10th September 1962, and completely from 13th July 1964.

7th August 1962

The Staines Branch

Plate 22
Colnbrook Estate Halt was a late addition to the branch, being opened on 1st May 1961. At that time, the future of the line must have looked secure; BR diesel multiple units were in use, these having displaced auto-trains and GWR railcars in October 1958. However, the passenger service was withdrawn from 29th March 1965.

6th August 1962

Plate 23
Situated roughly half-way along the branch, Colnbrook was the most important intermediate station. The crossing loop was put in during 1904 and extended in 1940, but the signal box was reduced to ground frame status in 1967. General freight ceased from 3rd January 1966, but steel and scrap metal traffic keep the line open.

6th August 1962

Plate 24
The development of a factory estate led to the opening of Poyle Estate Halt on 4th January 1954. Except in morning and evening rush periods, trains called only by request.
6th August 1962

Plate 25
Poyle Halt for Stanwell Moor was clearly an older structure, and it had opened on 1st June 1927. Originally called Stanwell Moor for Poyle, the name was changed from 26th September of the same year.
6th August 1962

Plate 26
Only a few concrete supports remain to mark the site of Yeoveney Halt, which closed from 14th May 1962. Originally opened to serve a rifle range at Runemede, under which name it first appeared in the timetable for 1892, the halt was renamed in 1935. Traces of a wartime connection to the Southern Railway can just be seen in the distance.

6th August 1962

Plates 27 & 28

At Staines (*above*) the original company adapted a private house for use as station accommodation. The suffix 'West' was added by BR in 1949 to distinguish it from the former SR station. As shown in the lower photograph, there was a large goods yard behind the long platform, but it closed from 2nd November 1953. On the opposite side, near the water tower, was a small engine shed, used for stabling two 0-4-2Ts from Southall Depot, until it closed in June 1952. Rather surprisingly, the signal box remained open until July 1959, when it was converted to a ground frame. An oil depot opened here in 1964, which brought additional traffic to the branch. In January 1981, a new connection from the SR Windsor branch was brought into use, which enabled part of the line between Staines and Colnbrook to be closed.

17th May 1959

Plate 29
Running into Iver at 5.40, 2-6-2T No. 6164 heads a through train from Paddington to Windsor. The station was opened on 1st December 1924, as a result of housing development in the area.

17th May 1959

Plate 30
The next train in the hourly Sunday service to Windsor is seen at Langley (Bucks), where a young enthusiast records 2-6-2T No. 6113. The station opened as Langley Marsh in 1845, became Langley in 1849; 'Bucks' was added in 1920 and dropped in 1975.

17th May 1959

Plate 31
The 8.05 semi-fast from Oxford to Paddington passes through Slough, hauled by 4-6-0 No. 6858 *Woolston Grange*. The signalman keeps an eye on the photographer, who had ventured off the platform end in order to include the East signal box in the picture.

18th May 1959

Slough

Plate 32
Slough Middle signal box, with 101 levers, was opened in 1905 and closed in October 1963, when track in the area was rationalised and Slough panel box was commissioned. The Windsor branch bears away to the left, past the engine shed.

18th May 1959

Plate 33
With a rather unusual leak from a steam cock, 2-6-2T No. 6120 brings in a train from High Wycombe, the 8.24 to Paddington, via Maidenhead. The story of how the Eton College authorities objected to a station at Slough is well-known, and the GWR had to wait until 1840 before a proper station could be erected. That was of Brunellian design having 'up' and 'down' platforms on the same side of the line, and the buildings shown date from 1884.

18th May 1959

Plate 34
The engine shed at Slough was erected in 1868, although it was modified in later years, and the lean-to was added when the GWR railcars were introduced in the mid-1930s. It had an allocation of some 45 locomotives, all tank engines, but tender engines could be seen as visitors. The code was SLO (GWR) or 81B (BR), and it was closed in June 1964. In this view from the Windsor direction, Nos. 4691, 9463, 9406, 3697 and 6134 are visible. Also present were Nos. 1450, 3608, 4638, 4650, 5766, 6133, 6151, 6152, 6167, 9421, 9424, 9781 and, stored out of use, No. 9722.

17th May 1959

To Windsor

Plate 35
After a few years, objections to a railway in Windsor became less vigorous, and an Act authorising a branch from the GWR at Slough was passed in 1848. It was opened on 8th October 1849 as broad gauge, and was made mixed gauge in 1862. The west-facing connection, shown here, was used mainly by Royal trains, and so was called the Queen's Curve. It was singled in 1963 and taken out of use in 1970.
5th August 1962

Plate 36
In 1883, the broad gauge rails were removed from the Windsor branch and the station was rebuilt. It was renamed Windsor and Eton in 1904, and the suffix 'Central' was added by BR in 1949. Here, 4-6-0 No. 5022 *Wigmore Castle* is seen backing out of the platform after working a Whit Sunday excursion from Wolverhampton. Although the goods yard closed from 6th January 1964, and only one platform remains in use, Windsor still has a good passenger service. Part of the station now houses an exhibition about Royalty and railways.
17th May 1959

The first section of the GWR, the 23 miles from Paddington to Maidenhead, was opened on Monday, 4th June 1838. On that day, 1,479 passengers were carried, and the takings amounted to £226. The western terminus was on the London side of the river, actually nearer to Taplow than Maidenhead, and had to serve both places until new stations were provided in 1872 and 1871 respectively. The next stretch of line, as far as Twyford, was opened on 1st July 1839.

Plate 37 (above left)
Hauled by 2-6-2T No. 6117, the 10.05 stopping train to Paddington arrives at Burnham (Bucks). The station consists of an island platform placed between the relief lines, and was opened in 1899 as Burnham Beeches. The name was changed in 1930, and the suffix was dropped in 1975. There was no goods yard here, and the signal box, seen on the far side of the main lines, closed in 1962.

18th May 1959

Plate 38 (left)
A Westbury engine, 4-6-0 No. 7924 *Thornycroft Hall*, speeds through Taplow at the head of a train conveying through carriages from Frome to Paddington, where it was due to arrive at 11.15. For a period in the mid-1960s Taplow goods shed was used as a base for the Reading Group of the Great Western Society, and several 'Open Days' were held here.

18th May 1959

Plate 39 (above)
The 12.55 express from Paddington to South Wales, with restaurant car to Swansea and through carriages to Carmarthen, passes through Maidenhead. At its head is 4-6-0 No. 4097 *Kenilworth Castle*, on its way home to Landore Shed. The station at this site was opened in 1871 and has four platform faces serving the main and relief lines, with a fifth for the branch trains, which once ran to and from High Wycombe.

17th May 1959

The Wycombe Railway was authorised in 1846 to construct a ten mile long branch from Maidenhead to High Wycombe. A broad gauge single line was opened on 1st August 1854, worked by the GWR, to whom it had been leased. The company amalgamated with the GWR in 1867, and the line was converted to standard gauge in the autumn of 1870. As the junction with the main line was over a mile beyond the original Maidenhead Station, the branch had its own station to serve the town, but it closed in 1871 when the junction station was opened.

To Bourne End

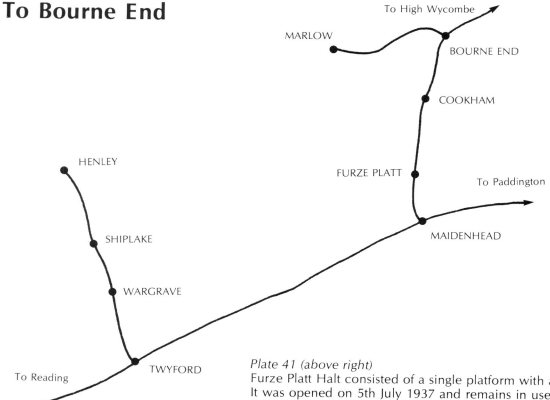

Plate 40 (below)
From the platform end, Maidenhead middle signal box and the goods shed can be seen. The three boxes here closed in December 1963 and were replaced by a new one which had a life of less than twelve years. The goods yard closed from 19th July 1965 and, on the right, the connections to the branch have been simplified.

17th May 1959

Plate 41 (above right)
Furze Platt Halt consisted of a single platform with a small ticket office. It was opened on 5th July 1937 and remains in use, although the term 'halt' was dropped in 1969. As 0-4-2T No. 1448 arrives with trailers W172 and W236, there are quite a number of passengers waiting, perhaps hoping to spend a pleasant day by the river.

17th May 1959

Plate 42 (below right)
On its way back to Maidenhead, No. 1448 arrives at Cookham, where a crossing loop was added in 1906. The loop was taken out in 1969, when the signal box was closed, and the level crossing gates have since been replaced by lifting barriers. The goods yard closed from 1st March 1965.

17th May 1959

Plates 43 & 44

When the Wycombe line opened, the town of Great Marlow was served by a station nearly three miles away, called Marlow Road. In 1874, by which time it was the junction for the Marlow branch, it was renamed Bourne End. This view *(above)* facing north, shows No. 1448 having just arrived from Maidenhead. On the right is the goods shed, which was closed from 11th September 1967. The passenger service from here to High Wycombe was withdrawn from 4th May 1970, when that part of the Wycombe branch closed completely. In the lower picture, No. 1448 can be seen setting off for Marlow. There was then a separate bay platform for Marlow branch trains, but the track here has been very much simplified.

17th May 1959

Plate 45
The branch from Marlow Road was opened on 28th June 1873, and was constructed by a nominally-independent company, the Great Marlow Railway. It was worked by the GWR and formal amalgamation took place in 1897. The station shown, with No. 1448 arriving from Bourne End, was closed from 10th July 1967, so that the site could be sold. A new platform was brought into use, situated on one of the former sidings in the goods yard, which had been closed from 18th July 1966.

17th May 1959

Marlow

Plate 46
In steam days, the branch train was affectionately known as 'The Marlow Donkey' and the engine, supplied from Slough, had its own shed. A notice, fixed to a leg of the water tower, stated that 4-6-0 engines must not enter this shed, but the only occupant at the time of the author's visit was a hedgehog. Closure was effected from 5th July 1962, when the branch service was dieselised.

17th May 1959

Plate 47
Running into the relief line platform at Maidenhead, 2-6-2T No. 6143 is working the 1.32 semi-fast train to Paddington.

17th May 1959

Plate 48
The 'up' 'Cornish Riviera Limited' was timed to leave Penzance at 10a.m. and arrive at Paddington at 5.20p.m., but on this Saturday, at the height of the holiday season, it was running late, and passed through Twyford at 6.20p.m. The first of the post-war 'Castles', No. 5098 *Clifford Castle*, is shown carrying a boiler fitted with the older-pattern tall chimney, which stood out against the evening sky.

11th August 1956

Twyford

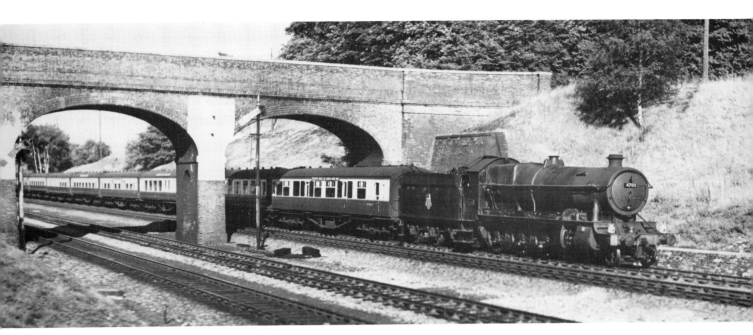

Plate 49
On summer Saturdays, the 47XX class of large-boilered 2-8-0s, which were normally used on fitted freight turns, were pressed into service on passenger duties. No. 4701 is seen approaching Twyford with the 5.05 Paddington to Weston-super-Mare; a train which made several intermediate stops and took 4¼ hours for the journey.

11th August 1956

Plate 50
Twyford Station had the usual four platform faces on the main and relief lines, plus a bay at the west end for Henley branch trains. Another Westbury engine is seen here, 4-6-0 No. 6951 *Impney Hall*, hauling through carriages from Trowbridge. This train would leave at 7.15 and call at most stations along the Berks & Hants route, and then run semi-fast from Reading to Paddington, where it was due at 10.38. At the end of the platform is the West signal box, and the goods shed is just visible; the latter closed from 7th September 1964.

17th May 1959

The Henley Branch

The single line branch from Twyford to Henley was opened on 1st June 1857. It was 4½ miles long, broad gauge, and had an intermediate station at Shiplake. Conversion to standard gauge took place in March 1876, and the track was doubled in 1898. In 1906, the first experiments in audible cab signalling were carried out on the Henley branch. More extensive trials on the Fairford branch led to the development of the GWR system of Automatic Train Control, whereby ramps placed between the rails were used to impart information to the driver on the position of distant signals, and also to apply the brakes if necessary.

Plate 51
A second intermediate station was opened on 1st October 1900, at Wargrave. It had two platforms, but only one remained in use after the line was singled in 1961.
17th June 1967

Plate 52
Shiplake had an island platform, and when the branch reverted to single line status, the crossing loop here was retained until 1969. The road level crossing is now an open one, and the goods yard, seen on the far side of it, closed when all goods traffic on the branch ceased in September 1964. Train movements over the branch have been controlled from Reading panel box since 1972.

7th August 1962

Plate 53
There were once three platforms at Henley-on-Thames, which was a veritable hive of activity at times, especially during Regatta Week. A small engine shed stood alongside, where modern housing now occupies the site of the yard. A pannier tank locomotive was normally supplied from Reading Shed until December 1958, shortly after the introduction of diesel multiple units.

17th June 1967

Plate 54
Passing through Sonning Cutting, 2-6-2T No. 6162, in unlined black livery, heads a typical semi-fast train of the period. Leaving Paddington's suburban platforms at 1.24p.m., it would make four stops and was due to arrive at Reading at 2.25p.m.

11th August 1956

Plates 55 & 56
Sonning Cutting, with its wooded slopes, was a popular spot for railway photographers, but the angle of the sun became very awkward for 'up' trains in the afternoon, producing deep shadows. Double-headed by two Gloucester-based 4-6-0s, Nos. 7006 *Lydford Castle* and 6917 *Oldlands Hall* *(above)*, the 11.45 from Cheltenham to Paddington would probably have commenced its journey behind a 2-6-2T. The 8.15 through train *(below)*, including restaurant car, from Perranporth to Paddington is hauled by an Old Oak Common engine, No. 6002 *King William IV*.

11th August 1956

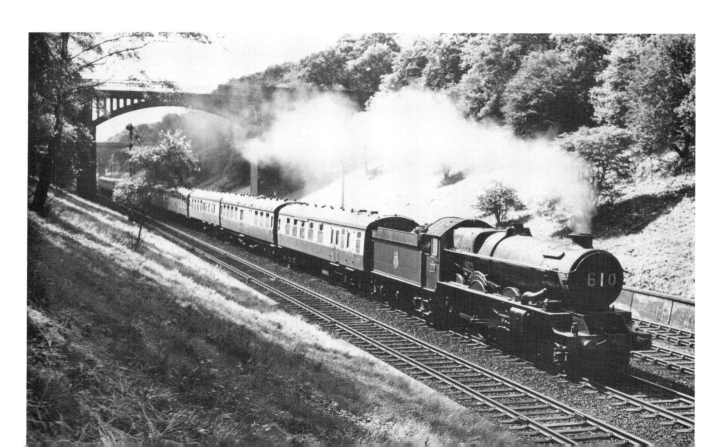

Reading

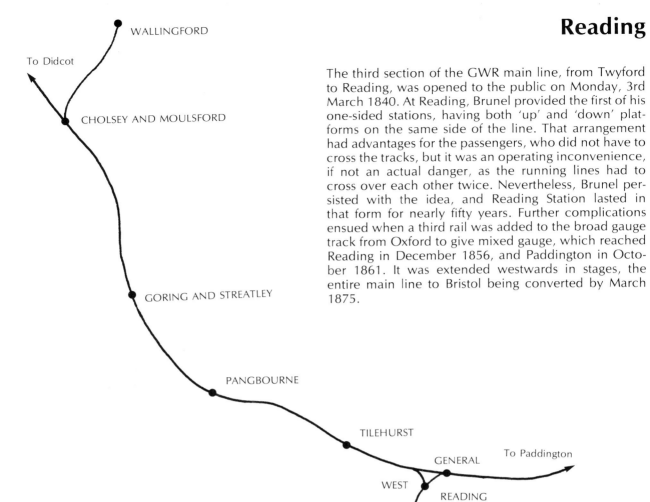

WALLINGFORD

To Didcot

CHOLSEY AND MOULSFORD

GORING AND STREATLEY

PANGBOURNE

TILEHURST

GENERAL

WEST

READING

To Paddington

To Plymouth etc.

The third section of the GWR main line, from Twyford to Reading, was opened to the public on Monday, 3rd March 1840. At Reading, Brunel provided the first of his one-sided stations, having both 'up' and 'down' platforms on the same side of the line. That arrangement had advantages for the passengers, who did not have to cross the tracks, but it was an operating inconvenience, if not an actual danger, as the running lines had to cross over each other twice. Nevertheless, Brunel persisted with the idea, and Reading Station lasted in that form for nearly fifty years. Further complications ensued when a third rail was added to the broad gauge track from Oxford to give mixed gauge, which reached Reading in December 1856, and Paddington in October 1861. It was extended westwards in stages, the entire main line to Bristol being converted by March 1875.

Plate 57
Painted green with black and orange lining, 2-6-2T No. 6150 waits to leave Reading (General) with a rake of 10 carriages forming the 12.12 to Paddington. From 6th September 1965, this station handled trains from the Southern Region, so that Reading (South) Station could be closed.

26th April 1959

Plate 58 (above)
Seen from the west end of Reading (General), an immaculate 'Castle' class 4-6-0, No. 5066 *Sir Felix Pole*, brings in the 8.50 express from Cheltenham. Fresh out of Swindon Works, No. 5066 had just been fitted with double blast-pipe and chimney. Put into traffic in July 1937 as *Wardour Castle*, it was renamed to commemorate the man who was General Manager of the GWR from 1921 to 1929. In a ceremony at Paddington Station on 24th April 1956, the new nameplate was officially unveiled by Mr John Pole, son of the late Sir Felix Pole. The engine was withdrawn from service in September 1962 and sold for scrap to John Cashmore Ltd., who cut it up in their yard at Great Bridge, Staffordshire.

26th April 1959

On 1st June 1840, the GWR opened the next section of the main line, from Reading to Steventon.

Plate 59 (above right)
Due to its position on the main line as a junction with the direct line to Plymouth and the Basingstoke branch Reading had an important engine shed with an allocation of nearly 100 locomotives and several diesel railcars. It was coded RDG (GWR) or 81D (BR), and officially closed to steam in January 1965. This view of the yard shows the three-bay straight road shed with the repair shop on the right. The engines identifiable are Nos. 4096 *Highclere Castle*, 6162 and 92245. Also on shed were Nos. 1407 2262, 2834, 2860, 3723, 3738, 4606, 4609, 4661, 4665 4670, 4707, 4917 *Crosswood Hall*, 4941 *Llangedwyn Hall* 4977 *Watcombe Hall*, 4987 *Brockley Hall*, 5010 *Restorme Castle*, 5036 *Lyonshall Castle*, 5322, 5973 *Rolleston Hall* 5982 *Harrington Hall*, 5993 *Kirby Hall*, 6110, 6122, 6126 6129, 6131, 6134, 6140, 6161, 6302, 6312, 6654, 6655 6842 *Nunhold Grange*, 6924 *Grantley Hall*, 6934 *Beachamwell Hall*, 6947 *Helmingham Hall*, 6953 *Leighton Hall*, 7327, 8430, 9402, 9447, 9749, 9791, 90323, 90693 and diesel-electric shunters Nos. 13195, 13196, 13268 and 13269.

26th April 1959

Plate 60 (right)
Reading (West), served by trains to Basingstoke and along the Berks & Hants line, was a station with a certain character of its own.

23rd August 1963

To Didcot

Plate 61 (above)
A lovely spring morning is just beginning to warm up as 4-6-0 No. 5901 *Hazel Hall* rolls into Tilehurst with the 10.49 train to Reading, on the last stage of its journey from Oxford. The station was opened in 1882.

26th April 1959

Plate 62 (below)
One of the original stations, Pangbourne later had four platform faces, but now only two remain in use.

22nd August 1963

Plate 63
Goring was another of the original stations, becoming Goring and Streatley in November 1895. The goods yard here, together with those at Tilehurst and Pangbourne, closed in September 1964.

22nd August 1963

Plate 64
Cholsey and Moulsford was opened in 1892 to replace an earlier station situated about three quarters of a mile nearer London. That was called Wallingford Road for a time, until a branch to serve the latter town was opened by the Wallingford & Watlington Railway on 2nd July 1866. It was the first standard gauge branch off the original GWR main line, and it never reached Watlington; it was formally absorbed in 1872. This view shows the Wallingford bay on the far left and 2-6-2T No. 6106 bringing a pick-up goods along the 'down' relief line. This engine is now preserved at the Didcot Railway Centre.

22nd August 1963

The Wallingford Branch

Plate 65 (above)
The branch auto-train was known locally as 'The Wallingford Bunk', and was photographed on a dull wet day, when it was worked by 0-4-2T No. 1444. Formerly a sub-depot of Didcot, Wallingford engine shed stands trackless, having closed from 11th February 1956. Branch passenger services were withdrawn from 15th June 1959 and freight from 13th September 1965, although most of the line remained open to serve a private siding until May 1981.

25th April 1959

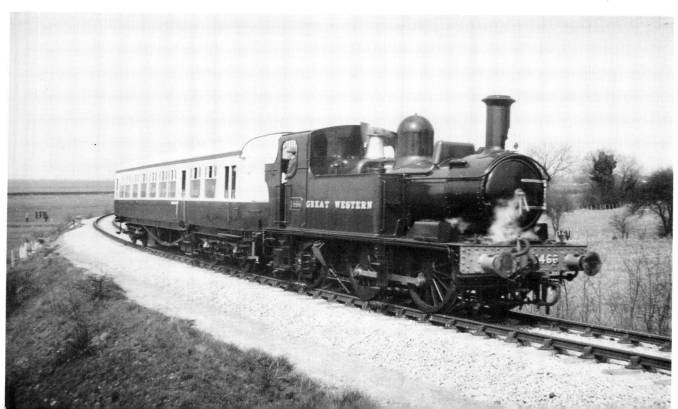

Didcot

Plate 67 (above)

The locomotive shed at Didcot is situated in the triangle formed by the curves to the Oxford line, and now forms part of the Didcot Railway Centre, home of the Great Western Society. The building shown was erected in 1932 and closed to BR steam in June 1965. Standing outside on this occasion were Nos. 3639, 2221, 5326 and 4915 *Condover Hall*.

25th April 1959

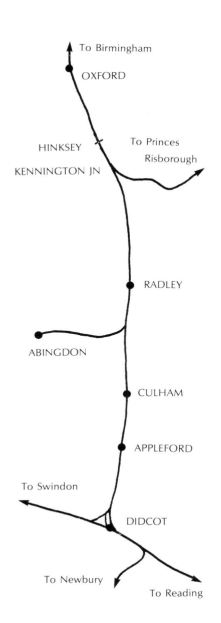

Plate 68 (above)

Coming round the west curve towards Foxhall Junction, 2-8-0 No. 3845 is hauling a typical mixed freight of the period.

22nd August 1963

Plate 66 (left)

It was a very different sort of day, some nine years later, when the Great Western Society was allowed to operate 0-4-2T No. 1466 and trailer No. 231 over the branch. Green paint and polished brass, chocolate and cream coachwork, all gleaming in the hazy sunshine, brought joy to the hearts of members and friends. The auto-train can still be seen at Didcot but, unfortunately, the tranquil atmosphere of that glorious afternoon can never be recaptured amongst the crowds at a preservation centre.

15th April 1968

Although an Oxford branch was included in the original GWR Prospectus, it did not materialise for several years, owing to opposition from local landowners and the University. It was authorised in 1843 and opened on 12th June 1844. There were intermediate stations at Appleford, which closed in 1849, and Abingdon Road, which was renamed Culham on the opening of the Abingdon branch. Worked by the GWR, the Abingdon Railway opened on 2nd June 1856, and ran from an exchange station named Abingdon Junction. Constructed to the broad gauge, conversion took place in 1872, but it remained single track. In 1873, the branch was extended for three-quarters of a mile alongside the Oxford line to a new station at Radley. The company was absorbed in 1904.

To Oxford

Plate 69
Appleford Halt, situated about two miles north of Didcot, was opened on 11th September 1933, and consists of wooden platforms and 'pagoda' waiting shelters. It remains in use, although it is no longer called a halt.

15th May 1965

Plate 70
The main station building at Culham is of Brunellian design but, in contrast, the signal box dates from 1952. It closed in February 1961, and access to the siding was provided by a ground frame until 1965. Running in with the 4.07 train to Oxford is 4-6-0 No. 5957 *Hutton Hall*.

26th May 1962

Radley for Abingdon

Plates 71 & 72
Just arriving in the bay platform of Radley Station, 0-4-2T No. 1442 (above) has brought a mixed train from Abingdon. The general view (below) of Abingdon Station yard shows the closed signal box on the right and the goods shed on the left. The small engine shed here, which used to house a locomotive supplied from Oxford, had closed in March 1954. At the buffer stop, No. 1442 and a trailer wait to leave at 12.55 for Radley. The Abingdon branch lost its passenger service from 9th September 1963, but private siding traffic kept this line in use until 1984.

25th April 1959

Plate 73
At Radley, there are several passengers for the 11.54 train to Didcot, hauled by a Banbury-based 4-6-0 No. 4964 *Rodwell Hall*. The station remains open, but goods traffic ceased in 1964 and the coal yard closed in 1971.

25th April 1959

Plate 74
Photographed near Kennington Junction, 2-8-0 No. 3830 is seen running without a safety valve cover, and in filthy condition, typical of steam locomotives in their last days.

15th May 1965

Plate 75
At Kennington Junction, the branch from Thame and Princes Risborough comes in. Originally built by the Wycombe Railway, it was opened throughout by 1864. Rather unusually, the signal box faces the branch, because at the time it was built, in 1901, there was a proposal to up-grade the branch to main line standard, but the work was never carried out. The 'up' 'Pines Express' is seen passing the junction, hauled by 4-6-0 No. 6967 *Willesley Hall*, running nameless. This train, which conveyed through carriages from Liverpool and Manchester to Bournemouth, was taken off its traditional route, via the Somerset and Dorset line, at the end of the summer timetable in 1962.

15th May 1965

Plate 76
A BR Standard Class 5 4-6-0, No. 73051, takes a Newcastle to Bournemouth train past Hinksey South signal box. The marshalling yard here, about a mile south of Oxford, was laid down in 1942 to assist in the war effort. For a short period, 1908-15, there was a halt here called Abingdon Road, and another at Hinksey, just over half a mile away.

15th May 1965

Plate 77 (left)
Viewed from the platform end, 4-6-0 No.
5960 Saint Edmund Hall is about to pass
Oxford Station South signal box.

11th June 1961

Plate 78 (below left)
The original Oxford terminus was
replaced by a new station in 1852. In its
later days, it had two through roads, two
platform roads and two bays at the north
end. After several years of slow deterio-
ration, rebuilding in modern style began
in 1970.

17th June 1967

Plate 79 (above)
Oxford engine shed had an allocation of about 60 locomotives, and
was situated on the 'down' side, north of the station. It was coded
OXF (GWR) or 81F (BR), and closed to steam in January 1966. An
evening view of 4-6-0 No. 5026 *Criccieth Castle* also shows two of the
2-8-2Ts which were based here. The following engines were recorded
during that visit: Nos. 1420, 1425, 2289, 2294, 3608, 3722, 3805,
4147, 4676, 4902 *Aldenham Hall*, 4903 *Astley Hall*, 4907 *Broughton
Hall*, 4921 *Eaton Hall*, 4933 *Himley Hall*, 4979 *Wootton Hall*, 5012
Berry Pomeroy Castle, 5413, 5808, 5922 *Caxton Hall*, 5965 *Woollas
Hall*, 6113, 6122, 6135, 6336, 6968 *Woodcock Hall*, 7008 *Swansea
Castle*, 7212, 7238, 7239, 7246, 7411, 7436, 7760, 9302, 9416, 9611,
9640, 9653, 9654, 44593, 48365, 61334, 64751, 75003, 75027,
80085, 90312, 90529 and railcar No. W15W.

11th September 1955

Plate 80
Built by British Railways in 1955,
bogie van No. W1037 stands near
Oxford goods shed and offices.
Originally designed for carrying
milk churns, but often used for
newspaper and parcels traffic, these
vans bore the telegraphic code
name of 'Siphon G'; possibly the
best known of all those used by the
GWR.

17th June 1967

Didcot

Plate 81
When the Oxford branch was brought into use, a station was opened at the junction, Didcot. It had an overall roof until damaged by fire in 1885, and further changes were made in 1932. The main line platforms are shown here, with 4-6-0 No. 7028 *Cadbury Castle* coming through with an 'up' express.

22nd August 1963

Plate 82
Photographed on Didcot Shed, 'Dean Goods' 0-6-0 No. 2532 was a veteran of 56 years, having entered traffic in June 1897, and it was destined to be withdrawn in May 1954. During 1905/6, it was on loan to the Manchester & Milford Railway for working improved services over the Aberystwyth to Carmarthen line, when it ran as M&MR No. 10.

9th August 1953

Didcot engine shed was coded DID (GWR) or 81E (BR) and had an allocation of about 50 locomotives. During a visit on 17th February 1952, the following were noted: Nos. 1334, 2202, 2221, 2222, 2240, 2532, 2826, 3024, 3043, 3211, 3622, 3709, 3721, 4318, 4326, 4649, 4935 *Ketley Hall*, 5350, 5380, 5381, 5735, 5744, 5752, 5903 *Keele Hall*, 5913 *Rushton Hall*, 5935 *Norton Hall*, 5962 *Wantage Hall*, 6112, 6116, 6118, 6910 *Gossington Hall*, 6952 *Kimberley Hall*, 7710, 9015 and 9417.

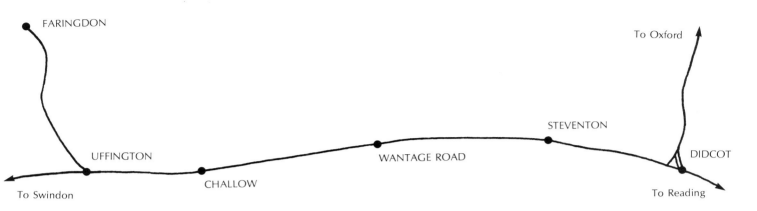

FARINGDON

To Oxford

STEVENTON

UFFINGTON

WANTAGE ROAD

DIDCOT

To Swindon

CHALLOW

To Reading

Plate 83
At Foxhall Junction, the west curve to the Oxford line, opened in 1886, goes off to the left. In the distance is Didcot Station, with the provender store prominent on the skyline. This building was erected in 1884 for the purpose of storing and blending hay, oats, maize, etc., to be sent out to all parts of the system as fodder for horses; about 3,000 of them were once employed for cartage and shunting. Each of the two towers carried a large water tank. The signal box shown was a 1931 replacement of the original, and was closed from 17th May 1965 as part of the multiple aspect signalling scheme for the main line. In the following years, MAS was extended along the line to Oxford, where a panel box was commissioned in 1973.

15th May 1965

Plate 84
For the first four years after it opened, Steventon was the station for Oxford, ten miles away. Following the abolition of separate London and Bristol Committees, for a period of about six months in 1842, meetings of the GWR Board of Directors were held in the large house seen in the background.

26th May 1962

Plate 86 (right)
As its name implied, Wantage Road was some distance from the town and, in 1875, a tramway was opened to bridge the intervening 2½ miles. A steam tram coach soon replaced the original horse-drawn passenger carriage and, in 1878, a locomotive was purchased from the LNWR for working goods traffic. It had been built by George England in 1857 for the Sandy & Potton Railway, and was named *Shannon*, but it became known as *Jane* on the Wantage Tramway. After the tramway had closed in December 1945, the little 0-4-0 well tank was bought by the GWR and restored at Swindon Works as WT Co. No. 5 *Shannon*. It was displayed on the platform at Wantage Road, as shown, until the station closed, when it was put into store before being given a home at the Didcot Railway Centre. After further restoration, it is capable of being steamed occasionally, and is now part of the National Collection.

26th April 1959

Plate 87 (below right)
The next section of the GWR was opened on 20th July 1840, as far as Faringdon Road, where the station was renamed Challow in 1864. On a running-in turn after overhaul in Swindon Works, 'Castle' class 4-6-0 No. 5085 *Evesham Abbey* calls with the 3.58 stopping train to Swindon. The station was modernised in 1933, when four tracks were in use from Wantage Road.

16th May 1959

Plate 85
Wantage Road Station opened in 1846, and the platform loops were added in 1932. This station, together with those at Steventon and Challow, closed completely when goods traffic ceased from 29th March 1965.

26th May 1961

Plate 88
The Faringdon Railway opened on 1st June 1864, running from a junction station at Uffington, and the company remained nominally independent until 1886. The layout at Uffington was modified in 1897, when the road overbridge replaced a level crossing, and the signal box shown was installed. A Swindon engine, 4-6-0 No. 5978 *Bodinnick Hall*, heads the 3.01 'up' stopping train. Those local passenger services, between Swindon and Didcot, were withdrawn from 7th December 1964. The signal box outlived the station, but it closed in March 1968.

16th May 1959

Plate 89
Branch trains had their own platform at Uffington, which was served by a loop off the main line. Beyond the platform can be seen the goods yard, with its loading dock and weighbridge office, and the stationmaster's house. The yard, together with the Faringdon branch itself, closed from 1st July 1963.

16th May 1959

Faringdon

Plate 90 (above)
This view of the terminus shows the engine shed, the chalet-style station building, and the goods shed on the right. The former, which used to house a small tank engine supplied by Swindon Shed until the passenger service was withdrawn from 31st December 1951, provides evidence of the branch's broad gauge origins. Conversion to standard gauge took place on 10th August 1878.

16th May 1959

Plate 91 (below)
The Railway Enthusiasts' Club of Farnborough ran a special train over the branch, worked from Reading by rather unusual motive power, 0-6-0ST No. 1365. The special is shown at Faringdon, ready for the return trip.

26th April 1959

Plate 93 (below)
The stretch of line from Faringdon Road to Wootton Bassett Road, about three miles beyond Swindon and sometimes called Hay Lane, was opened on 17th December 1840. The intermediate station, Shrivenham, was modified in 1933 when the platform loops were added, and it closed from 4th October 1965, when goods traffic ceased. Passing through with the 10.28 from Swindon to Paddington is 4-6-0 No. 5932 *Haydon Hall*.

1st May 1960

late 92 (left)
Io. 1019, *County of Merioneth*, a Swindon-based 4-6-0
ocomotive, takes a 'down' express through Uffington.
16th May 1959

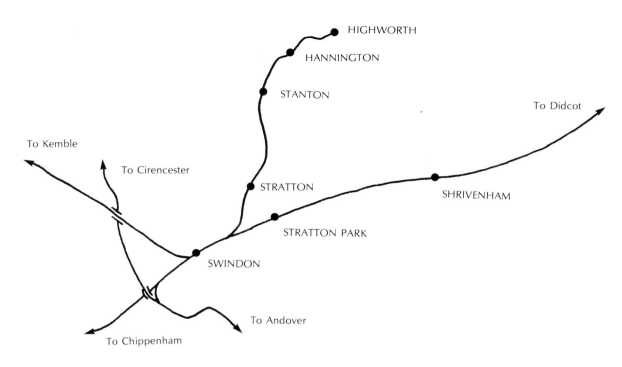

HIGHWORTH

HANNINGTON

STANTON

To Didcot

To Kemble

To Cirencester

STRATTON

SHRIVENHAM

STRATTON PARK

SWINDON

To Andover

To Chippenham

Plate 94
Situated on the main line just over two miles east of Swindon, Stratton Park Halt was opened on 20th November 1933.
On a dull Sunday morning, 'Castle' class 4-6-0 No. 5090 *Neath Abbey* comes bustling through with the 8.00 buffet car
train from Weston-super-Mare to Paddington.

3rd May 1959

The Highworth Branch

An Act incorporating the Swindon & Highworth Light Railway Company was passed on 29th June 1875, and construction began in 1879, but the total funds needed to build a line to the standard necessary to satisfy the Board of Trade could not be raised from local sources.

Consequently, the company was taken over by the GWR, who carried out the required improvements and opened the five and a half mile long line on 9th May 1883.

Plate 95
The first station on the branch served the village of Stratton St. Margaret. Access to the goods loop was controlled by two ground frames in later years, the signal box having closed in 1909. The goods yard, by then used for coal traffic only, closed in 1965, when the line beyond the first mile was put out of use. All has since been swept away by site redevelopment.

3rd May 1959

Plate 96
There was once a small goods yard behind the platform at Stanton, but the station closed from 2nd March 1953, when the passenger service was withdrawn.

1st May 1960

Plate 97
Only the platform remained at Hannington, where there had once been a goods loop and siding in the space on the right.

1st May 1960

Plate 98
This view, facing the buffer stop at Highworth, shows that even here the station building was of timber construction. It was to a design used by the company engineer, Arthur Pain, on several lines with which he was associated. Workmen's trains continued to run over the branch after the end of public passenger services, but all traffic here ceased from 6th August 1962, when the branch closed beyond Kingsdown Road, where the siding to the former Vickers Armstrong factory diverged.

1st May 1960

Swindon

Even before this section of railway was opened to traffic, the GWR Directors, acting on the advice of Brunel and his Locomotive Superintendent, Daniel Gooch, resolved 'That the Principal Locomotive Station and Repairing Shops be established at or near the junction with the Cheltenham and Great Western Union Railway at Swindon'. The Works were brought into regular use on 2nd January 1843, and new engines began to emerge in 1846, of which the first to be built entirely at Swindon was a 2-2-2 named *Great Western*. Carriage and Wagon Shops were later erected and the Works grew in size until about 12,000 persons were employed there. Living accommodation was provided by the Company in early days, and a new town grew up between the railway and Old Swindon.

Plate 99
The 'Castle' with the longest nameplate, No. 5069 *Isambard Kingdom Brunel*, is about to pass Swindon East signal box with the 5.00 restaurant car express from Paddington to Weston-super-Mare. Opposite the box is its intended replacement, which was never commissioned, as the older one was retained until Swindon panel box came into use in March 1968.
30th April 1960

Plate 100
Illuminated by a brief spell of sunshine after a thunderstorm, 4-6-0 No. 4940 *Ludford Hall* was recently ex-works in the BR livery for mixed traffic locomotives of black, lined out in red, cream and grey. For a period of a few months, the name and numberplates of former GWR engines had the background painted red. Shed plates had not then come into general use, so the code SBZ for St. Blazey was stencilled on the footplate angle iron.
17th March 1950

Plate 101
Platforms to allow passengers to change trains existed in 1841, but the permanent buildings, including the famous refreshment rooms, were not opened until the following year. An unidentified train bound for the Gloucester line comes through the station, hauled by 'Castle' class 4-6-0 No. 5084 *Reading Abbey*. The locomotive, which began its life in 1922 as a member of the 'Star' class, is seen fitted with a double chimney, a four-row superheater, and a Davies & Metcalfe mechanical lubricator. The station has changed considerably; passenger traffic is concentrated on the former 'up' island platform, and a modern office block stands on the site of the old entrance building on the 'down' side.

3rd May 1959

Plate 102
Selected passenger classes were painted Brunswick green by British Railways, and lined out in a manner similar to, but not quite the same as, that of the GWR. Red-painted plates on green engines looked even more garish, and the practice soon ceased. A Worcester-based 'Castle' No. 5063 *Earl Baldwin*, illustrates the style described.

17th March 1950

The excitement engendered by a visit to Swindon Works and shed in steam days was a result of not knowing what would be seen — the freshly painted gleaming engines, perhaps brand-new or modified in some way; the rare engines from distant sheds; or the veterans at the end of their working lives. On the following pages is a representative selection of photographs taken on such visits. At the time of writing, the Works, already reduced in size and importance, is under threat of complete closure.

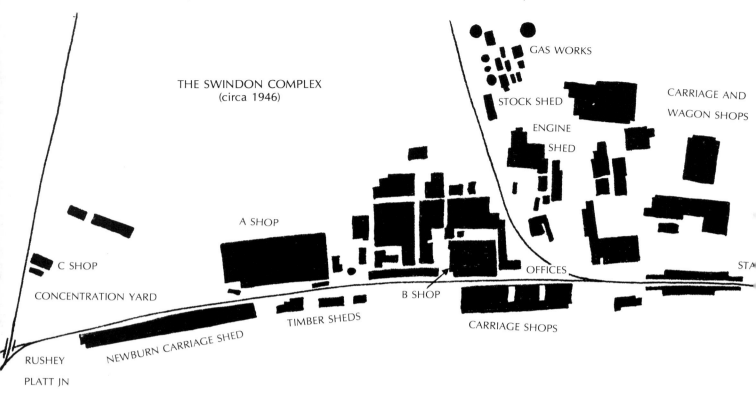

THE SWINDON COMPLEX
(circa 1946)

GAS WORKS

STOCK SHED

ENGINE
SHED

CARRIAGE AND
WAGON SHOPS

A SHOP

C SHOP

CONCENTRATION YARD

OFFICES

B SHOP

STA

TIMBER SHEDS

CARRIAGE SHOPS

NEWBURN CARRIAGE SHED

RUSHEY

PLATT JN

Plate 103
This view from the platform end has the West signal box and its clock as the most prominent feature. To the left are the old carriage shops, in the centre are the main works offices and on the right are the smithy, offices and stores of the wagon works. The engine shed is out of sight, round the curve of the Gloucester line.

1st July 1964

A broad gauge shed had existed at Swindon since 1842, but one for standard gauge locomotives was opened in 1871. It was originally a straight shed with nine roads, but a turntable was installed, and a large roundhouse was added in 1908. Coded SDN (GWR) or 82C (BR), it had an allocation of just over 100 engines, and it closed to steam in November 1965. A visit on 22nd April 1956, found the following engines present: Nos. 1000 *County of Middlesex*, 1019 *County of Merioneth*, 1371, 1400, 1462, 1658, 2852, 2879, 3614, 3645, 3684, 3724, 3746, 3763, 3829, 4289, 4573, 4612, 4902 *Aldenham Hall*, 4925 *Eynsham Hall*, 4928 *Gatacre Hall*, 4953 *Pitchford Hall*, 4972 *Saint Brides Hall*, 4993 *Dalton Hall*, 5000 *Launceston Castle*, 5062 *Earl of Shaftesbury*, 5063 *Earl Baldwin*, 5068 *Beverston Castle*, 5081 *Lockheed Hudson*, 5351, 5396, 5509, 5536, 5540, 5566, 5721, 5800, 5805, 5931 *Hatherley Hall*, 5972 *Olton Hall*, 5975 *Winslow Hall*, 6306, 6630, 6639, 6737, 6741, 6850 *Cleeve Grange*, 6912 *Helmster Hall*, 6956 *Mottram Hall*, 7418, 7792, 7903 *Foremarke Hall*, 7923 *Speke Hall*, 8433, 8461, 8783, 9476, 9600, 9720, 9772, 9795 and 75009.

Plate 104
Standing in the shed yard are Nos. 5922 *Caxton Hall*, 2873 and 3822; the latter is now preserved at Didcot. No. 5068 *Beverston Castle* is just inside the straight-road shed, and part of the roundhouse roof is visible on the right.

28th May 1961

Plate 105
A Swindon-based engine, 4-6-0 No. 5975 *Winslow Hall*, waits its turn at the coaling stage.

3rd June 1956

Plate 106
After nationalisation, during the interim period when the work of designing BR Standard locomotives was carried out, the various regions continued to build to the old companies' designs. So it was that the final batch of 'Castles' was not built until 1950, and No. 7037 was the last of a long line of GWR 4-cylinder 4-6-0s. It was officially named *Swindon*, in a ceremony performed at the Works by the then Princess Elizabeth on 15th November, to commemorate the Golden Jubilee of the Borough. No. 7037 is shown at Swindon Shed, where it was allocated at the time, although that was not always the case. It was withdrawn in March 1963 and sold for scrap, eventually being cut up by John Cashmore Ltd. at Newport.
22nd April 1956

Plate 107
In April 1958, 0-6-0PT No. 3711 was converted to burn fuel oil instead of coal, at the works of Robert Stephenson & Hawthorn Ltd., using equipment supplied by Messrs Laidlaw Drew. The experiment appears to have been successful, although no further conversions were made. No. 3711 was subsequently based at Old Oak Common or Swindon, and is shown in the small roundhouse of the latter shed.

1st May 1960

Plate 108
The GWR ceased building 0-6-0 tender engines in 1899, but construction to a new design began in 1930, with the object of releasing some of the 'Dean Goods' engines from main line duties so that they could be used on the Cambrian Section. Built in June 1938 and withdrawn in June 1960, No. 2297 was a visitor to Swindon from Banbury. Behind it is 4-6-0 No. 5922 *Caxton Hall*.

4th May 1958

Plate 109
Diesel railcar No. W21W and 4-6-0 No. 5067 *St. Fagans Castle* were dumped on a siding which ran from the gasworks towards the rear of the shed. They had been withdrawn in August and July 1962 respectively. At the end of their working lives, some of these railcars were used as personnel carriers, taking permanent way gangs to site.

26th April 1963

Plate 110 (left)

At the rear of the running shed was the engine stock shed, used for storing locomotives which were temporarily surplus to requirements. Standing outside are Nos. 9012 and 9018, two of the 4-4-0s once known as 'Earls'. The former, then running as No. 3212 *Earl of Eldon*, was the last one to be given nameplates, and all were removed in 1937, to be fitted to 'Castles'. Also in store were Nos. 2289, 4003 *Lode Star*, 5009 *Shrewsbury Castle*, 5802, 5806, 5812, 5814, 5817, 5819, 7413, 7794, 8472, 8779, 9005, 9009, 9011 and 9023. In the background is the retort house of the GWR gasworks, which commenced production on that site in 1876, and was enlarged over the years until it was reputedly the largest in the world in private ownership. It closed down in 1959.
22nd April 1956

Plate 112 (above)
The tremendous amount of hard work done by members of the 'Star' class, the first GWR 4-cylinder 4-6-0s, tends to be neglected by present-day writers, and the class has been overshadowed by the later 'Castles' and 'Kings'. Fortunately, in 1951, the 'powers that be' selected No. 4003 *Lode Star* for preservation. One of the first batch built in 1907, the engine was kept in the stock shed, minus name and numberplates, until Swindon Museum was ready to receive it in 1962.
16th June 1957

Plate 111 (below left)
GWR No. 5 was an 0-6-0T named *Portishead* which was acquired from the defunct Weston, Clevedon & Portishead Railway in 1940. After several years' use on light shunting duties, in 1950 it was placed in the stock shed, where it remained until it was condemned four years later.
18th April 1952

Plate 113 (below)
In the early 1960s, numerous withdrawn locomotives were stored in the vicinity of the gasworks, awaiting cutting up or sale for scrap. However, of the two shown here, 0-6-0PT No. 1621 was condemned, but 2-6-2T No. 6159 was in use as a stationary boiler, and had another two years of active life left.
28th April 1963

Plate 114 (above)
Engines sent to the Works were first placed in the reception sidings, known as the Triangle. Standing in front of the Chief Mechanical & Electrical Engineer's offices is No. 1153, an 0-4-0ST acquired from Messrs Powlesland & Mason, haulage contractors in Swansea Docks. It was built by Hawthorn Leslie & Co. Ltd., Works No. 2258, and supplied to Sir Alfred Hickman's Spring Vale Furnaces, Bilston, Staffs, in 1903, where it was named *Dorothy*. It was sold to P&M in 1919 and passed into GWR hands in 1924, becoming No. 942 and losing its name. A new boiler was fitted in 1926, and it was renumbered 1153 in 1949. The reason why it was at Swindon is rather unusual. Shunting duties at Reading Signal Works were normally carried out by a Simplex petrol locomotive, but both those available locally had broken down, so No. 1153 was transferred from Danygraig. As it was necessary for the engine to enter the shops, it soon made itself unpopular by filling the air with smoke and fumes. As soon as the petrol shunter was repaired, No. 1153 was sent off to Swindon, where it spent several months in the stock shed. It returned to Swansea in January 1954 for a final spell of shunting in the docks before being withdrawn and cut up at Caerphilly in October 1955. Even then, its boiler was sent back to Danygraig for stationary use.

14th June 1953

Plate 115 (above right)
Although it had been withdrawn from normal service in October 1954, 0-6-2T No. 322 was still in use as a Works shunter, and is seen taking a Sunday rest from its labours. Behind it is BR Standard 2-6-2T No. 82019, built at Swindon in September 1952. In the background is the stripping shed, known as the Barn. No. 322 was re-numbered from 441 in 1947, and was previously Taff Vale Railway No. 120 of Class A, designed by John Cameron in 1912. The 58 engines were built by four different companies; No. 120 was Hawthorn Leslie No. 3062 of 1914. They had the reputation of being poor steamers and, after they had passed into GWR hands at the Grouping, they were reboilered. In 1923, No. 120 was sent to Swindon and fitted with a GWR Standard No. 10 boiler, then given extensive trials before the others were dealt with.

24th April 1955

Plate 116 (right)
For shunting the more sharply curved sidings of the Wagon Works area, a short wheelbase engine was necessary, and 0-6-0PT No. 1369 was one of a class of five built in 1934 for that purpose. It also saw service on Weymouth Quay and on the Wenford Bridge branch in Cornwall before withdrawal in November 1964. No. 1369 is now preserved on the Dart Valley Railway. In the background are the gable ends of the roof of 'A' Shop.

24th April 1955

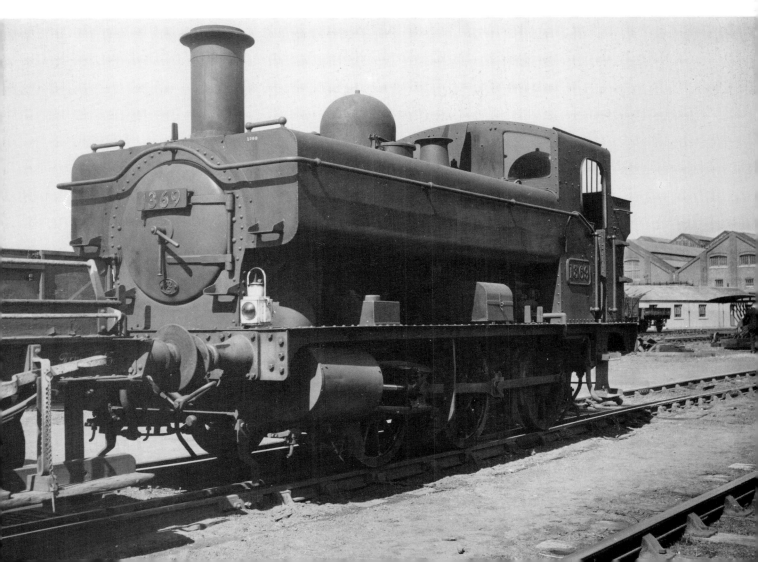

Plates 117 & 118
Undoubtedly the pride of the Works was the magnificent 'A' Shop; 11½ acres of covered accommodation. The first 5¾ acres were opened in stages from 1901 to 1903, and the area was almost doubled in 1921. It then comprised four sections: Erecting Shop, Machine and Fitting Shop, Boiler Shop and Wheel Shop. They were laid out to enable locomotive repairs to be carried out in a progressive sequence. The later part contained 60 pits 100ft. long, an electric traverser and four 100 ton overhead cranes of 75ft. span. Two photographs illustrate the interior of 'A' Erecting Shop. One shows No. 6993 *Arthog Hall,* 6025 *King Henry III* and 2892 over the pits *(above)* and the other *(above right)* shows the traverser with No. 6023 *King Edward II* identifiable on the far side.

1st May 1960

Plate 119 (right)
Tucked away in 'A' Shop was a bench devoted to the cleaning and polishing of locomotive nameplates. Those on the bench are from No. 1020 *County of Monmouth,* while those underneath include plates from Nos. 7008 *Swansea Castle,* 6014 *King Henry VII,* 6007 *King William III,* 6858 *Woolston Grange* and 4909 *Blakesley Hall.* The men who worked at that bench would never have realised how the value of the items which they were handling was going to soar in later years. Any plate is now worth several hundred pounds to a collector and some have been sold for four figure sums. Also in the Works at this time were Nos. 1026 *County of Salop,* 1428, 1449, 1612, 2265, 2832, 2833, 2840, 2865, 2880, 3794, 3859, 4079 *Pendennis Castle,* 4080 *Powderham Castle,* 4096 *Highclere Castle,* 4377, 4584, 4663, 4703, 4904 *Binnegar Hall,* 4931 *Hanbury Hall,* 4972 *Saint Brides Hall,* 5015 *Kingswear Castle,* 5019 *Treago Castle,* 5233, 5355, 5523, 5989 *Cransley Hall,* 6016 *King Edward V,* 6018 *King Henry V1,* 6020 *King Henry IV,* 6023 *King Edward II,* 6027 *King Richard I,* 6104, 6137, 6141, 6330, 6366, 6814 *Enborne Grange,* 6823 *Oakley Grange,* 6993 *Arthog Hall,* 7013 *Bristol Castle,* 7019 *Fowey Castle,* 7035 *Ogmore Castle,* 7301, 7437, 7740, 7761, 7788, 8762, 8799, 41294, 41299, 46505, 46507, 46513, 46514, 75007, 75021, 75023, 78002, 78007 and diesel-electric shunters Nos. 13000, 15100 and 15102. New construction consisted of BR Standard 2-10-0s, of which No. 92087 was almost complete.

29th July 1956

On the Triangle and in the Works Yard area, on 29th July 1956, were Nos. 44, 303, 316, 377, 394, 1001 *County of Bucks*, 1027 *County of Stafford*, 1647, 2270, 2861, 2892, 3038, 3042, 4903 *Astley Hall*, 4989 *Cherwell Hall*, 4991 *Cobham Hall*, 5001 *Llandovery Castle*, 5049 *Earl of Plymouth*, 5065 *Newport Castle*, 5092 *Tresco Abbey*, 5094 *Tretower Castle*, 5191, 5571, 5996 *Mytton Hall*, 6001 *King Edward VII*, 6012 *King Edward VI*, 6156, 6821 *Leaton Grange*, 6975 *Capesthorne Hall*, 7415, 7435, 7828 *Odney Manor* and 7903 *Foremarke Hall*. Some of those were just ex-works, others were awaiting Works and some would be cut up. Former TVR 0-6-2Ts Nos. 312, 348, 351, 382 and 389 were in use as Works shunters. Also present was new 0-6-0PT No. 3407, just delivered from the Yorkshire Engine Company, who had built it as sub-contractors to the Hunslet Engine Company. It was to be condemned in October 1962 after a life of only six years. Nos. 5316 and 5327 were down in the Concentration Yard for scrapping.

Plate 120
'Castle' class 4-6-0 No. 5077 *Fairey Battle* stands in the Works Yard, resplendent in lined green livery with the more appropriate black plates. When built, in August 1938, the engine was named *Eastnor Castle*, but it was renamed in October 1940 as one of a series commemorating World War II aircraft. It was withdrawn in July 1962 and sold for scrap to Messrs R. S. Hayes of Bridgend.

13th June 1954

Plate 121
As an example of the BR engines built at Swindon, here is Class 3 2-6-0 No. 77011 just out of the shops in mixed traffic livery of lined black. Next to the buffer stop is coal-weighing tender No. 4128, one of two built in 1952; the last ones of a non-standard design to be constructed at Swindon.

13th June 1954

Plate 122
In 1956, the Western Region authorities decreed that certain mixed traffic engines hitherto painted black could now be painted green and lined out. Pictured standing outside the Iron Foundry, 4-6-0 No. 7912 *Little Linford Hall* must have been one of the first to be given the new livery. The letters ID stencilled behind the buffer beam indicate improved draughting and, like No. 5077, No. 7912 was fitted with three-row superheater and mechanical lubricator. The engine was built in March 1950 and withdrawn in October 1965.
3rd June 1956

Plate 123
Some locomotives which would have been plain green in GWR days were lined out by British Railways, and 4-6-0 No. 7828 *Odney Manor* was the first of its class to be so treated. Another engine built by BR to a GWR design, No. 7828 entered traffic in December 1950 and was withdrawn in October 1965, later being rescued from Barry Scrapyard for preservation at Toddington.
27th July 1956

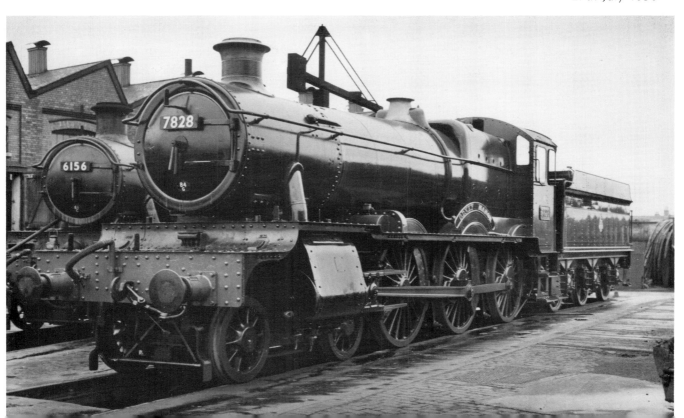

Plate 124 (above)
Outside the engine preparation shed of 'A' Shop, three condemned 4-6-0s await sale for scrap. The first two went to Woodham's Yard at Barry, from where No. 6024 *King Edward I* was rescued for preservation. No. 6023 *King Edward II* may also be preserved, but No. 4086 *Builth Castle* was cut up by John Cashmore Ltd.

9th September 1962

Plate 125 (left)
The GWR ordered a gas turbine locomotive from the Swiss firm of Brown-Boveri in 1946, but it was not delivered until February 1950. In December 1960, No. 18000 was withdrawn, and eventually returned to Switzerland, where it was used as a mobile laboratory. It still survives, and is now in Vienna.

1st May 1960

Plate 126 (right)
Locomotives for scrapping were sent to the Concentration Yard, otherwise known as the Dump. Here is a group from an older generation, comprising the remains of 4-6-0 No. 2954 *Tockenham Court*, former Rhymney Railway 0-6-2T No. 73, 4-6-0 No. 4023, once named *Danish Monarch*, and 2-6-2T No. 5144.

24th August 1952

Plate 127
This memorable line of condemned engines on Swindon Dump included 'Star' 4-6-0 No. 4058 *Princess Augusta*; the last of the once numerous Wolverhampton-built saddle tanks, No. 1925; two 'Bulldog' 4-4-0s, No. 3447 *Jackdaw* and 3451 *Pelican*; 'Star' 4-6-0 No. 4018 *Knight of the Grand Cross*; 0-6-0PT No. 1993; 'Bulldog' 4-4-0 No. 3377, once named *Penzance*; 'Star' 4-6-0 No. 4041 *Prince of Wales*; and former Barry Railway 0-6-2T No. 274.

20th May 1951

Plate 128
No. 2001 built at Wolverhampton Works in December 1891 as a saddle tank, was converted to a pannier tank in August 1911, and withdrawn in August 1952 after more than 60 years' service. In August 1948, it was painted green and lettered 'BRITISH RAILWAYS', the last engine to be finished in that style at Wolverhampton.

24th August 1952

Plate 129
In 1932, a large shed was erected at the end of the Concentration Yard to facilitate the breaking up of condemned engines, and it became known as 'C' Shop. The cutting torch produces a shower of sparks from 0-6-0T No. 2165, formerly Burry Port & Gwendraeth Valley Railway No. 12. It was built by Hudswell Clarke in 1913, Works No. 1024, and was condemned in March 1955.

24th April 1955

Plate 130
The GWR produced a new class of 4-4-0 locomotive in 1936 by fitting 'Duke' type boilers to 'Bulldog' frames. Although the resulting product looked antiquated, it was a relatively cheap way of producing lightweight engines for certain restricted lines, particularly the Cambrian Section. Named *Earl of Ducie*, No. 3211 entered traffic in March 1937, but the plates were removed a few months later. In 1946 renumbering to 9011 took place, and the locomotive was withdrawn in July 1957.

25th August 1957

Plate 131
GWR No. 82 was formerly Rhymney Railway P class 0-6-2T No. 4, built by Robert Stephenson & Co. in 1909, Works No. 3372. It was fitted with a GWR Standard No. 10 taper boiler in 1926, the first engine to be so modified at Caerphilly Works. Originally a passenger engine, No. 82 ended its days on shunting duties, and was withdrawn in May 1954.

13th June 1954

Plate 132
For many years, the engines to be found in 'C' Shop were veterans from the GWR and pre-grouping companies but, inevitably, the time came when what were thought of as modern locomotives were seen there. Built in 1936, 4-6-0 No. 6802 *Bampton Grange* was withdrawn in August 1961 from Pontypool Road Shed.

10th September 1961

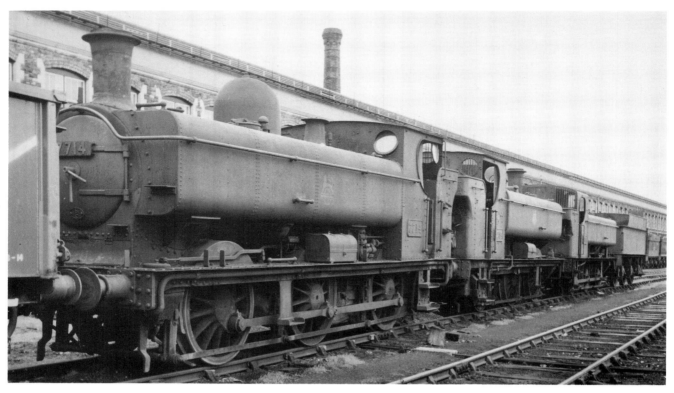

Plate 133
These three withdrawn pannier tanks, standing in the Works Yard, were sold to the National Coal Board, and were destined to see further use at collieries in South Wales. The first two, Nos. 7714 and 7754, were subsequently purchased for preservation, but No. 1600 was eventually scrapped.
3rd May 1959

Plate 134
On the same day, a long line of engines was photographed on the Dump. It included Nos. 2812, 2830, 5743, 2254, 6727, 4584, 4377, 2833, 5388, 2825, 6428, 6409, 4226, 4261, 2828 and 6355. Most, if not all, of those were also sold, but to scrap metal firms for breaking up.
3rd May 1959

Plate 135 (above)
No. 3186, built in January 1908 and
withdrawn in June 1957, illustrates
the large-boilered type of 2-6-2T.
The majority of the class were
allocated to Severn Tunnel Junction
for pilot duties through the tunnel,
but this one came from Laira Shed.
16th June 1957

Plate 136 (above)
Withdrawn in June 1962, 4-6-0 No.
6008 *King James II* was languish-
ing on the Dump, but its nameplate
would be given a home by some
fortunate collector.
9th September 1962

Plate 137
During the closing period of steam
on British Railways, it was rather
odd that although the Western
Region was selling most of its own
condemned locomotives for scrapping by outside firms, several LNER
V2s should be sent to Swindon for
cutting up. On the Dump are Nos.
60887, 60932 and 60964, formerly
named *The Durham Light Infantry*.
20th September 1964

To Kemble

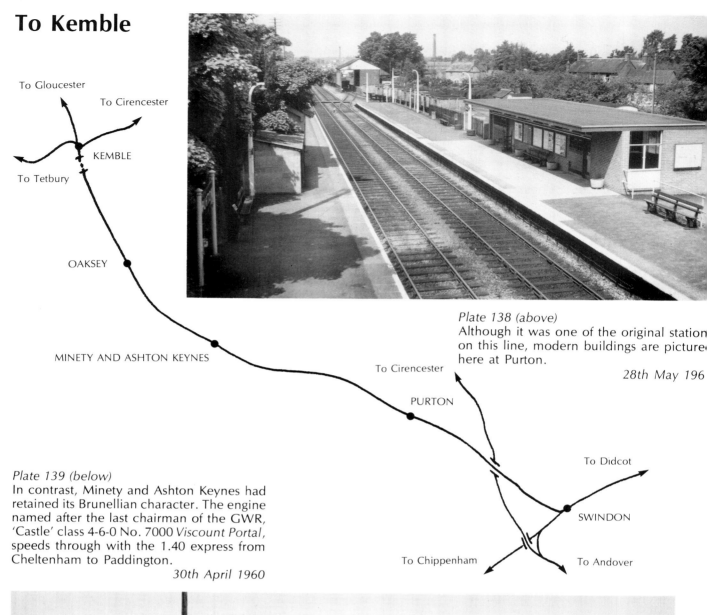

To Gloucester

To Cirencester

KEMBLE

To Tetbury

OAKSEY

MINETY AND ASHTON KEYNES

To Cirencester

PURTON

To Didcot

SWINDON

To Chippenham

To Andover

Plate 138 (above)
Although it was one of the original station
on this line, modern buildings are picture
here at Purton.

28th May 196

Plate 139 (below)
In contrast, Minety and Ashton Keynes had
retained its Brunellian character. The engine
named after the last chairman of the GWR,
'Castle' class 4-6-0 No. 7000 *Viscount Portal*,
speeds through with the 1.40 express from
Cheltenham to Paddington.

30th April 1960

Plate 140
Oaksey Halt was opened on 18th February 1929. It closed from 2nd November 1964, as did Purton and Minety stations.

21st August 1963

Plate 141
The Cheltenham & Great Western Union Railway was authorised by an Act of 1838, leased to the GWR in 1840, and purchased outright in 1843. The line from Swindon to Kemble and on to Cirencester was opened on 31st May 1841. In early days, Kemble had only an exchange platform for use by Cirencester passengers, and the station shown did not appear in the timetable until 1872. This was to comply with the wishes of a local landowner, who also insisted that the line should be enclosed in a tunnel where it passed his residence, Kemble House.

18th August 1962

West of Swindon

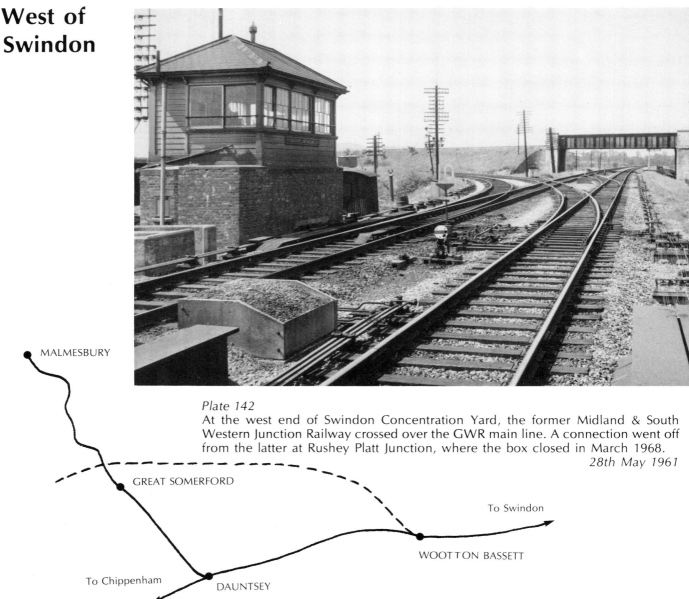

MALMESBURY

GREAT SOMERFORD

To Chippenham

DAUNTSEY

WOOTTON BASSETT

To Swindon

Plate 142
At the west end of Swindon Concentration Yard, the former Midland & South Western Junction Railway crossed over the GWR main line. A connection went off from the latter at Rushey Platt Junction, where the box closed in March 1968.
28th May 1961

The Malmesbury Branch

Plate 143 (left)
he next section of the GWR, from
ay Lane to Chippenham, opened
n 31st May 1841. A station at
Wootton Bassett was brought into
se a few months later, but it did
ot become a junction until the
adminton route was opened. No.
369, a Churchward 2-6-0, is seen
assing through, light engine.
losure to passenger traffic took
lace from 4th January 1965, and to
oods from 4th October of the same
ear.
28th May 1961

Plate 144 (above)
Dauntsey Station was opened in February 1868, and on 17th
December 1877 it became the junction for the Malmesbury Railway.
Branch trains used a bay at the end of the 'up' platform, and
underneath the arch of the road bridge can be seen the signal box,
which stood in the junction fork. The goods yard, sited at the
opposite end of the station, closed in June 1963, and complete
closure was effected from 4th January 1965.
19th August 1961

Plate 145 (right)
There was an intermediate halt at
Great Somerford, but it closed on
17th July 1933, when a connecting
curve was opened to the Badminton
line at Little Somerford. The timber
platform was dismantled and the
line to Dauntsey put out of use, but
the station house, formerly the
crossing keeper's cottage, survived,
and is now a private residence.
28th May 1961

Plate 146
The Malmesbury Railway was a nominally independent company which was absorbed by the GWR in 1880, although the 6½ mile long line was worked by the latter from its opening on 17th December 1877. This view of the terminus shows the small engine shed which used to house a locomotive supplied from Swindon; 0-4-2T No. 5806 being the occupant in 1950. It closed when the passenger services were withdrawn from 1st September 1951, but the building survives in the midst of a small industrial estate. The branch was closed completely from 12th November 1962.

4th May 1958

Plate 147
Christian Malford Halt, situated between Dauntsey and Chippenham, opened on 18th October 1926 to serve a village about half a mile away. It closed from 4th January 1965, when local trains between Swindon and Bristol were withdrawn.

19th August 1961

Chippenham for Calne

Plate 148 (above)
Chippenham was one of the original stations, but it was modified and enlarged over the years. It had three platform faces, of which two now remain in use. An enamelled sign read 'Junction for Calne, home of Harris', referring to the firm of bacon curers and manufacturers of sausages, pies, etc. The 11.05 train from Wolverhampton to Weymouth is pictured running in behind 4-6-0 No. 6930 *Aldersey Hall.*

19th August 1961

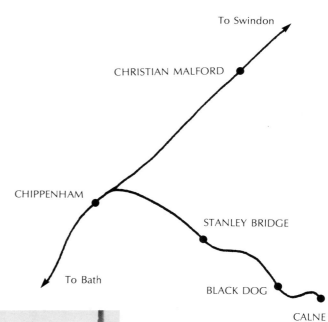

To Swindon

CHRISTIAN MALFORD

CHIPPENHAM

STANLEY BRIDGE

To Bath

BLACK DOG

CALNE

Plate 149
A Swindon-based pannier tank, No. 3645, brings a train of open wagons past the goods shed; a reminder of the days when such transfer trips were worked on Saturday afternoons. There were numerous sidings here which were taken out of use over the years, and freight facilities were finally withdrawn in January 1981.

19th August 1961

The Calne Branch

Members of the Harris family were amongst the promoters of the Calne Railway, another nominally independent company, whose line was worked by the GWR and formally absorbed in 1892. The first train, on 29th October 1863, brought pigs and merchandise, chiefly coal, but passenger trains began on 3rd November. The 5¼ mile long branch was originally broad gauge, and was converted to standard gauge during the weekend of 15th and 16th August 1874. Passenger services became diesel-operated in 1959, and were withdrawn from 20th September 1965. The branch was then closed completely, as goods traffic had ceased from 2nd November 1964.

Plate 150
Chippenham East signal box, the turntable and shed yard, can be seen here, with 4-6-0 No. 6968 *Woodcock Hall* standing nearby. This was not the type of engine allocated to the shed, which would have had about nine tank engines supplied from Swindon. It closed on 2nd March 1964. The Calne branch diverged to the right, opposite the shed.

17th August 1963

Plate 151 (below)
Stanley Bridge Halt was opened on 3rd April 1905, and once had a shelter to protect the numerous milk churns handled here.

27th July 1961

Plate 152
In 1874, a platform was erected at Black Dog for the use of the Marquis of Lansdowne. Members of the public were also allowed to use it, although it did not appear in the timetable until September 1952. It even had a stationmaster until 1930 but it was unstaffed from 1st February 1960. A ground frame gave access to a siding which served the Lansdowne Estate and a local coal merchant, but these facilities were withdrawn in June 1963.

27th July 1961

Plate 153
This view of the terminus gives some indication of the extensive freight and parcels traffic once handled at Calne. The goods shed is on the right, with a loading dock and siding into the premises of Messrs C. & T. Harris, situated further over. A small engine shed, situated near the end of the platform, had closed in the 1890s.

27th July 1961

The section from Chippenham to Bath was opened on Wednesday, 30th June 1841 and, by linking up with the previously opened line to Bristol, completed the main line of the Great Western Railway. That notable event appears to have taken place without any public ceremony, although a Directors' special ran from Paddington to Bristol and on to Bridgwater over the Bristol & Exeter Railway.

Plate 154 (left)
Just over 2 miles past Chippenham the Westbury line diverges at Thingley Junction. This view, facing Chippenham, shows the West signal box, which was opened in September 1943 when the junction was made triangular. Air Ministry sidings occupied the space on the left, but all was taken out of use in 195 and trees can be seen growing on the site of the west curve.

19th August 196

Plate 155 (below)
At Corsham, another of the original stations, the main building was above platform level. General goods traffic ceased in June 1963 and complete closure took place from 4th January 1965.

19th August 1961

This section included the heaviest engineering works on the entire line, not least of which was the tunnel through Box Hill. Work began in 1836 by sinking trial shafts, and contracts were let in 1838 for the tunnel proper. Nearly a hundred men are said to have lost their lives during its construction. For most of its length it passed through various clays, and it was brick lined; the remainder passed through Bath stone, or great oolite, and was largely unlined. It is 3,212 yards long and falls from east to west on a gradient of 1 in 100.

Plate 156

Emerging from the west portal of Box Tunnel, 4-6-0 No. 4993 *Dalton Hall* heads the 1.18 semi-fast train from Paddington to Weston-super-Mare. The tunnel mouth was made larger than the actual bore, and was ornamented with stonework to impress both rail and road travellers, as it was visible from the turnpike road to Bath. The oft-repeated story that the sun's rays shine directly through the tunnel on Brunel's birthday, 9th April, was checked by the personal observation of Mr D. J. Stuart. He reported in the 1974 *Journal of the Stephenson Locomotive Society* that the phenomenon did occur, but not until about a week after the quoted date.

28th August 1958

Plate 157 (above)
An empty stock or parcels train, hauled by 2-6-0 No. 6334, approaches Box Tunnel and passes the overgrown Pictor's Siding, where a short length of baulk road was still in situ.

28th August 1958

Plate 159 (above)
After passing through the 198yd. long Middle Hill Tunnel, the line emerged at Box Station, where the original Brunellian building can be seen. Stone was loaded into wagons from the dock opposite, and there was once a shed sited near the water tank to house a banking engine, but it closed in 1909. Goods traffic ceased in June 1963.
19th August 1961

Plate 158 (left)
Box (Mill Lane) Halt was opened on 1st March 1930, and was better sited to serve the village than the earlier station had been. Running in with the 4.57 local train to Bristol is 0-6-0 No. 2232.
19th August 1961

Plate 160 (right)
Bathford Halt, opened on 18th March 1929, was only about three-quarters of a mile from Bathampton, but it was situated by a main road junction and was convenient for the nearby village. Box Station, Mill Lane and Bathampton halts all closed from 4th January 1965.
19th August 1961

Plate 161
On a fine Sunday morning when many people would be thinking of travelling in the opposite direction, 4-6-0 No. 5040 *Stokesay Castle* takes the 8.00 Weston-super-Mare to Paddington express through Bathampton. Opened in 1857, the station lost its goods facilities in June 1963, and was unstaffed from 4th January 1965, but did not close completely until 3rd October 1966.

6th June 1960

To Trowbridge

Plate 162
From a road bridge over the Westbury line, Thingley Junction and the main line to Bath can be seen in the distance. In February 1967, single line working was introduced between Thingley and Bradford junctions.

19th August 1961

The Wilts, Somerset & Weymouth Railway Company was formed in 1844, with GWR assistance, to build a broad gauge line from near to Chippenham through Frome, Yeovil and Dorchester to Weymouth, with branches to Devizes, Bradford, Salisbury, Radstock, Sherborne and Bridport. In 1846, a further Act authorised, amongst other things, an extension from Bradford to join the GWR at Bathampton. The line from Thingley Junction to Westbury was opened on 5th September 1848, but the company then found itself short of capital and was taken over by the GWR in 1850. Construction of the remainder of the line proceeded in stages over a number of years.

Plate 163
On 16th October 1905, the GWR opened a halt at Lacock, about a mile from Thingley Junction. In 1943, several sidings were laid down for the Air Ministry and, to control access to these and Thingley West Curve, a new signal box was erected. The sidings and the box were taken out of use in 1964 and the halt closed from 18th April 1966. It is interesting to note that, in the year of the birth of the GWR, at nearby Lacock Abbey, William Henry Fox Talbot was carrying out experiments which led to his invention of the negative-positive process of photography.

6th June 1960

Plate 164
Two more halts were opened a fortnight later, one each side of Melksham, at Beanacre and Broughton Gifford. Both closed from 7th February 1965. Here is the site of Beanacre Halt, where there was a signal box and a siding into a War Department depot from 1939 to 1948.

6th June 1960

Plate 165 (above)
As passengers wait for a local train to Chippenham, 4-6-0 No. 6879 *Overton Grange* passes through Melksham with empty stock. Melksham was one of the original stations on the WS&W line, and developed into a busy railhead with private sidings for several local firms. However, as a result of the gradual drift of traffic away from rail, general freight facilities were withdrawn from 2nd November 1964, and passenger services from 18th April 1966. Derelict platforms, the goods shed and a few rusty sidings remain in situ, but only a single running line sees regular use now.

6th June 1960

Plate 166 (above right)
The branch to Devizes was opened on 1st July 1857, diverging from th WS&W line near the village of Holt. An exchange platform was provide at the junction, but it did not appear in the timetable until 1861. In Jun 1874, the line from Thingley Junction and that from Devizes wer converted to standard gauge. Also in that year, local residents wer permitted to join the trains at Holt Junction, which they reached by footpath across the fields. In 1877, a proper road was built to serve th station, and a goods shed was erected. Improved accommodatior including a ladies' waiting-room, was provided in 1875. A covered loadin bay, for the milk traffic of Nestle's of Staverton, was erected in 1909, an a station house in 1923. The 1950s and 1960s brought a decline; genera goods traffic ceased from 7th October 1963 and passenger services fror 18th April 1966, when the line to Devizes closed completely. Holt Junctio has gone, but its memory is preserved in two fascinating booklets produce by the *Holt Magazine*, which describe the effect that the coming of th railway had upon a village community.

6th June 196

Plate 167 (right)
Staverton Halt was opened on 16th October 1905 in the form of lo platforms, typical of those provided for the steam railmotors which th GWR was introducing at that time. Platforms of standard height and waitin shelters were provided a few years later. Closure was effected from 18t April 1966, when local passenger services between Chippenham an Trowbridge were withdrawn.

6th June 196

Plate 168 (left)
The second intermediate stati
on the Westbury line was at Tro
bridge, the county town of W
shire. It remains open, although
importance is much diminishe
and general freight traffic ceased
July 1967. The running shed he
which opened in 1875, closed
1923, when the allocation of abc
25 engines was transferred
Westbury.

19th August 19

Via Bradfor

Plate 170 (right)
Avoncliff Halt, nestling in the valle
of the River Avon, was opened o
9th July 1906. Both Avoncliff an
Freshford remain open, althoug
unstaffed, to serve rather isolate
communities.

6th June 196

Plate 169 (below)
Bradford did not get its railway until 2nd February 1857, when a
single line was opened from a junction about 1¼ miles north of
Trowbridge to Bathampton on the main line. This view of the station,
called Bradford-on-Avon from 1899, shows the 159yd. long tunnel
which lies to the east of it. The goods yard closed in November 1965.

6th June 1960

Plate 171 (below)
Freshford was one of the original stations, but had been modernised. Goods traffic ceased in June 1963 and the signal box closed shortly afterwards.

6th June 1960

Plate 172
On a rather dull evening, 4-6-0 No. 4947 *Nanhoran Hall* arrives at Limpley Stoke with the 5.26 'up' local train, a through working from Bristol to Portsmouth. Another of the original stations, Limpley Stoke suffered a slow decline; it closed to goods in January 1960, was unstaffed from March 1961 and closed completely from 3rd October 1965. From May 1910, a branch went off from the west end of the station to Camerton, linking up with a line from Hallatrow. It was put out of use in stages, but a stretch remained as a siding until 1960.

28th August 1958

Plate 173
At Bathampton Junction, a new signal box had been erected in 1956, but it closed in 1970. In spite of the complications of mixed gauge pointwork, very few accidents seem to have resulted from this, but one occurred here on 11th June 1875. The branch from Bradford Junction had been converted to standard gauge in June 1874, and a broad gauge train failed to negotiate the junction correctly, causing the leading carriage to overturn.

6th June 1960

The Bradford branch was doubled in 1885 and the junction was made triangular in 1895. Although under threat of closure in recent years, the northern curve is part of a useful diversionary route when the main line through Box Tunnel is closed, so it will probably be retained, and the branch will be singled through to Bathampton.

Plate 174
'The Merchant Venturer' was the name given in 1951 to the 11.15 express from Paddington to Weston-super-Mare, which served Bath and Bristol en route, although the return train made several more stops and took significantly longer for the journey. Shown here arriving at Bath, the 'down' train is hauled by 4-6-0 No. 6003 *King George IV*. Originally possessing an overall roof, the station was completely rebuilt in 1897, and was called Bath Spa in later years. The elevated signal box, which was such a prominent feature, closed in January 1968.

28th August 1958

Plate 175
In the early days, there was an engine shed near the station, but it was closed in 1880 and was replaced by another at the end of the goods yard on the Bristol side of the city, shown here almost opposite Bath Goods signal box. It used to house a pannier tank for shunting duties, and the 2-6-2T off the last train of the day from Bristol, Nos. 3765 and 5547 on 10th February 1957, from St. Philip's Marsh and Bristol (Bath Road) sheds respectively. It closed in February 1961.

20th August 1961

Bath to Bristol

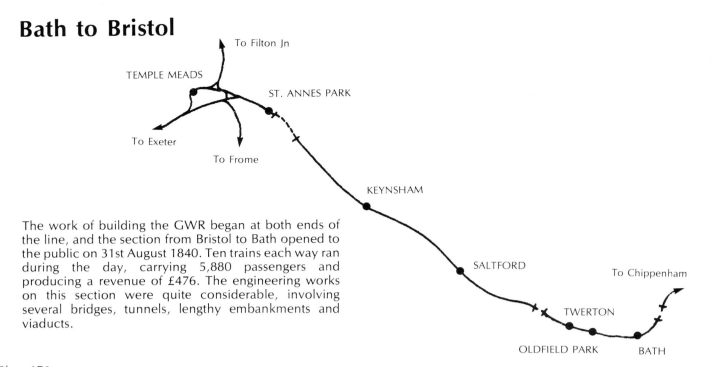

The work of building the GWR began at both ends of the line, and the section from Bristol to Bath opened to the public on 31st August 1840. Ten trains each way ran during the day, carrying 5,880 passengers and producing a revenue of £476. The engineering works on this section were quite considerable, involving several bridges, tunnels, lengthy embankments and viaducts.

Plate 176
A Sunday morning train from Bristol to Weymouth rolls into Oldfield Park at 10.10, behind 4-6-0 No. 1014 *County of Glamorgan*. Only one mile from Bath, the station was opened on 18th February 1929, with fairly basic facilities and no goods yard. It became unstaffed in October 1969.

20th August 1961

Plate 177 (above)
Twerton Station was opened in December 1840 and renamed Twerton-on-Avon on 1st August 1899. It closed in April 1917, as did Hampton Row Halt on the London side of Bath. The station building, shown here from the roadside, has been used for various commercial purposes, the current one being the spares department of the Morris Minor Centre; another reason why it interests the author.
18th August 1963

Plate 178 (below)
Saltford also opened in December 1840, but it survived as a passenger station until 5th January 1970. In 1909, the platforms were extended and the goods sidings were brought into use, but the latter closed in September 1959. The 176yd. long tunnel can just be seen in the distance.
5th June 1960

Plate 179 (above)
On the opening day, Keynsham was the only intermediate station between Bristol and Bath, as is once again the case. The name was changed to include Somerdale in 1925, and changed back in 1974. The goods yard was closed in November 1965, station staff were withdrawn in 1969, and the buildings have been demolished.

5th June 1960

Plate 180 (below)
The 11.15 local train to Bath runs into St. Anne's Park, and 2-6-2T No. 5536 is duly noted by the lads on the platform. This station opened in 1898, was unstaffed from March 1967, and closed completely from 5th January 1970, when local services between Bristol and Bath were withdrawn.

24th August 1958

Plate 181
This panoramic view shows the extent of the marshalling yard at Bristol East Depot, and the variety of wagons handled there at that time. The yard was brought into use in 1890 to deal with increasing goods traffic, particularly that resulting from the opening of the Severn Tunnel in 1886. The elevated signal box on the right was replaced in 1960, but the new box had a life of only ten years due to the Bristol MAS scheme which was introduced in 1970. An unidentified 'Hall' heads an 'up' excursion.

24th August 1958

Plate 182
Beyond Bristol East Depot Down Yard signal box the running lines cross over the River Avon. On the far side, the Bristol relief line curves away to the left; it was opened in 1892 to provide a means of bypassing Bristol (Temple Meads) Station.
18th August 1963

Temple Meads

Plate 183
Rounding the curve on the approach to Bristol (Temple Meads), 4-6-0 No. 6015 *King Richard III* brings in the 11.15 restaurant car express from Paddington to Taunton. At first, there were separate stations here for the Bristol & Exeter and GW companies, with a platform on the connecting line between them. Later, the Bristol & Gloucester Railway, which joined the Midland Railway, used the GW terminus. The first rebuilding took place in the late 1870s.

5th June 1960

Plate 184
The original engine shed near Bristol (Temple Meads) Station belonged to the B&ER, but shortly after that company was absorbed by the GWR in 1876, the latter closed their own shed at South Wales Junction and moved here. The B&ER workshops were converted to a standard gauge running shed, and piecemeal additions were made over the years. In the early 1930s, the old buildings were demolished and a new ten-road running shed was erected. It had an allocation of almost 100 engines for passenger duties and a few shunting turns, as freight duties were covered by St. Philip's Marsh Shed. It was coded BL by the GWR, changed to BRD in later years, and 82A by BR, and closed to steam in September 1960. Here is the well-known view of the shed yard as seen from the platform, showing the coaling stage with the repair shop behind it, and the usual pall of smoke hanging around the main building. The following were noted during a visit on 18th May 1952: Nos. 1002 *County of Berks*, 1007 *County of Brecknock*, 1014 *County of Glamorgan*, 1028 *County of Warwick*, 1415, 2818, 2954 *Tockenham Court*, 3676, 3737, 3795, 4056 *Princess Margaret*, 4060 *Princess Eugenie*, 4091 *Dudley Castle*, 4096 *Highclere Castle*, 4521, 4535, 4539, 4577, 4592, 4595, 4603, 4930 *Hagley Hall*, 4942 *Maindy Hall*, 4961 *Pyrland Hall*, 5012 *Berry Pomeroy Castle*, 5019 *Treago Castle*, 5048 *Earl of Devon*, 5078 *Beaufort*, 5096 *Bridgwater Castle*, 5506, 5511, 5512, 5514, 5535, 5546, 5555, 5559, 5572, 5771, 6102, 6374, 6900 *Abney Hall*, 6915 *Mursley Hall*, 6967 *Willesley Hall*, 6982 *Melmerby Hall*, 6995 *Benthall Hall*, 7917 *North Aston Hall*, 8795 and 9604.

5th June 1960

Plate 185
Another familiar view, this time from the Bath Road itself, shows the south end of the station with 4-6-0 No. 5037 *Monmouth Castle* passing by light engine, about to go on shed. The roof of the B&ER offices can be seen on the left skyline. Colour-light signalling was installed, and the platforms on the right added during the 1930s rebuilding, which was necessary to deal more efficiently with trains of both the GW and LMS Railways.
5th June 1960

Plate 186
When photographed alongside the platform at Bristol (Temple Meads), Bath Road-based 4-6-0 No. 7019 *Fowey Castle* was just over a year old, and was fated to have a working life of just under 16 years. The frame attached to the smokebox door was used for carrying train identification numbers.
11th July 1950

The Badminton Route

Plate 187

A new line, 31 miles long, from Wootton Bassett to the Severn Tunnel line north of Bristol, called the South Wales & Bristol Direct Line, was authorised in 1896. It opened to passenger traffic on 1st July 1903, thus shortening the route to South Wales by ten miles, as well as providing an alternative route to Bristol. There were seven stations on the new line, the first one being at Brinkworth, which closed completely when local passenger services between Swindon and Filton Junction were withdrawn from 3rd April 1961.

28th May 1961

Plate 188 (below)

The new line crossed the Malmesbury branch and the River Avon by means of a viaduct near the Somerfords, but not for another 30 years was a permanent connection made with the branch. On 18th July 1933, Little Somerford became the junction for Malmesbury, and trains ran to and from the 'up' platform loop, which was signalled for working in either direction. The goods yard here closed in June 1963.

28th May 1961

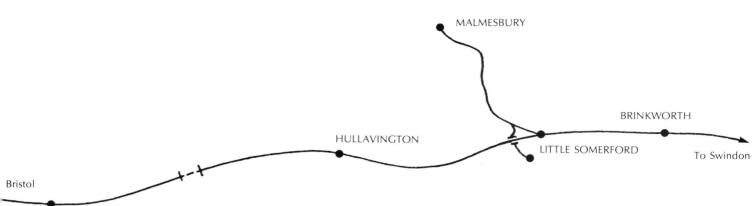

MALMESBURY

BRINKWORTH

HULLAVINGTON

LITTLE SOMERFORD

To Swindon

Bristol

BADMINTON

Plate 189 (right)
Hullavington Station closed completely when goods traffic ceased in October 1965.

27th July 1961

Plate 190 (below)
Badminton was provided with a fairsized station, platform loops and a goods yard, not visible in this westfacing view. The latter closed in November 1966. After the withdrawal of local passenger services, a few expresses between London and South Wales continued to call, as the agreement with the Duke of Beaufort which allowed the GWR to build the line across his land also entitled him to a train service. Nevertheless, the station closed completely from 3rd June 1968.

20th August 1963

Plate 191
After passing through the 4,444yd. long tunnel under the Cotswolds, the line reached Chipping Sodbury, another once busy country station. General goods traffic ceased in June 1966.

4th June 1960

Plate 192
On 1st May 1903, the GWR opened a connecting line from a triangular junction at Westerleigh, on the Badminton route, to Yate on the Midland Railway line to Gloucester. Here is Westerleigh East Junction, with the curve out of use and overgrown.

4th June 1960

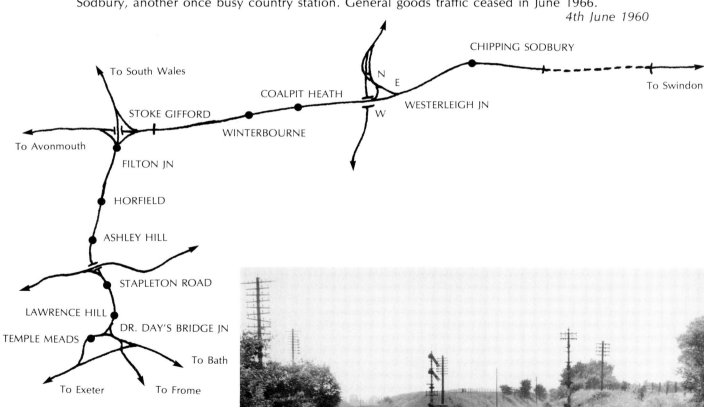

Plate 193 (above)
Seen passing Westerleigh Junction signal box, 'Britannia' class Pacific No. 70022 *Tornado* hauls the 1.55 express from Paddington to West Wales; one of the trains which called at Badminton. The west curve drops down to the left.
4th June 1960

Plate 194 (left)
The two curves come together at Westerleigh North Junction, where the signal box closed from 4th January 1950, when the east curve was taken out of use for the fourth and final time. It had previously been out of use from 1907 to 1908, 1916 to 1918, and 1927 to 1942. Track was left in situ in case it should be required again, but it was lifted about fifteen years later.
4th June 1960

Plate 195 (right)
Beyond the junction, the running lines divide, the north-bound one going straight ahead to cross the MR line by a flyover before joining it. Both curves were closed in 1907 due to a dispute with the MR, then reopened in 1908, and a new service between Wolverhampton and Bristol began to travel via Westerleigh on 2nd November. As a result of the closure of the former MR route to Bristol from Yate, the flyover was rendered unnecessary, and from 18th January 1970, both tracks followed the same path.
4th June 1960

Plate 196 (above)
The name of Coalpit Heath is a reminder of the mining activity that was the reason for building Bristol's first railway; a horse-worked tramway from here to a wharf on the River Avon, which opened on 6th August 1835. The station closed completely from 3rd April 1961.

4th June 1960

Plate 197 (below)
Winterbourne was the last of the seven stations on the new line, and it survived for goods traffic until October 1963.

4th June 1960

Plate 198
A new marshalling yard was laid down at Stoke Gifford, where the lines to Bristol and South Wales parted company, and were later joined by one from Avonmouth. For some sixty years it was the centre of great activity, but its use gradually diminished and much of it was closed in October 1971. The site of the 'up' yard, seen here to the right of Stoke Gifford West signal box, was used for a new station, which opened on 1st May 1972. At first called Bristol North, it was renamed Bristol Parkway, and has proved to be very popular.

27th June 1964

Plate 199
The Badminton line joined that from South Wales at Filton Junction, where a new station was opened, replacing an earlier one on the Bristol side of the road bridge. A few wagons and a brake van from Stoke Gifford Yard trundle through behind 0-6-0PT No. 3795.

4th June 1960

Plate 200
The 1903 station had four platforms, and the author was standing on the wrong one when a famous engine turned up on the 6.47 to Bristol, a local train from Swindon. On 9th May 1904, 4-4-0 No. 3440 *City of Truro* became the first steam locomotive in the world to achieve a speed of 100m.p.h. as it descended Wellington Bank on an 'Ocean Mails' special from Plymouth. After being withdrawn in March 1931, *City of Truro* was sent to York Railway Museum where it remained until January 1957, when it was brought out and restored to working order. It was used on enthusiasts' specials and local workings from Didcot or Swindon. In May 1961, it was again withdrawn and, later, placed in Swindon Railway Museum, but *City of Truro* will be out working again in the GWR Sesquicentenary Year.

4th June 1960

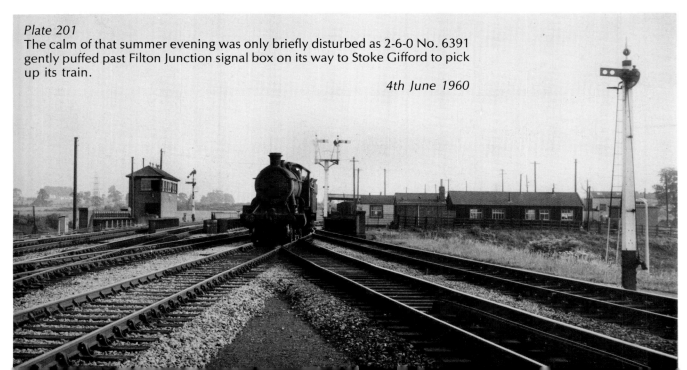

Plate 201
The calm of that summer evening was only briefly disturbed as 2-6-0 No. 6391 gently puffed past Filton Junction signal box on its way to Stoke Gifford to pick up its train.

4th June 1960

Plates 202 & 203
The Bristol & South Wales Union Railway was authorised in 1857 and opened as a broad gauge single line from South Wales Junction, about a quarter of a mile to the east of Bristol (Temple Meads) Station, to New Passage Pier, from where a ferry service operated to the Monmouthshire bank of the river. It was converted to standard gauge in August 1873, and doubled throughout by 1887. Horfield Platform (above) was opened in May 1927, and the suffix was dropped in 1933. Ashley Hill (below) opened in 1864 and a goods yard was provided in 1924, which closed in November 1966. Both stations closed to passengers from 23rd November 1964.

18th August 1963

Plate 204
A station at Bristol (Stapleton Road) was brought into use when the line opened, but alterations were made when the section northwards was quadrupled in 1888. It was once considered to be the exchange station for South Wales trains, but is now of less importance, and general freight traffic ceased in November 1965. Standard 2-6-2T No. 82044 is seen arriving with the 4.37 to Bristol from Severn Beach.
24th August 1958

Plate 205
Similarly, Lawrence Hill was one of the original stations, and was altered when the line to Dr. Day's Bridge Junction was quadrupled in 1891. A local train from Avonmouth Dock due here at 5.05, but running a few minutes late, is worked by 2-6-2T No. 5508.
24th August 1958

Plate 206
Late in 1958, diesel multiple units appeared in the Bristol area and, in the following months, began displacing steam from local passenger services. Even so, it was several years before steam locomotives disappeared entirely; the last ones being based at Bristol (Barrow Road), the former LMS shed. A Standard 2-6-2T, No. 82001, is seen coasting down through the cutting towards Dr. Day's Bridge Junction, a few months before the end. In February 1984, the line from here to Filton Junction was reduced to two tracks once more.

5th July 1965

Plate 207
In happier days, 2-6-2T No. 5561 was photographed performing station pilot duties at Bristol (Temple Meads). It is shown emerging from beneath the overall roof which was erected by the GWR in 1874.

5th June 1960

Plate 208
With a light haze drifting from the chimney, and a wisp of steam showing at the safety valve, 4-6-0 No. 6025 *King Henry III* glides through Twyford with the 8.20 express from Penzance to Paddington. The subdued exhaust beat and seemingly effortless progress hide the skill and artistry of the men on the footplate. Cumulus clouds gather as the sun sinks lower in the sky, and another memorable afternoon by the lineside draws to a close.

11th August 1956

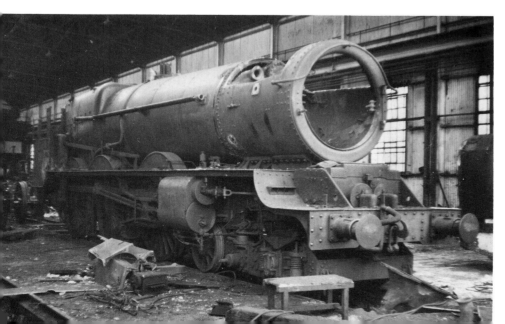

Plate 209
Regular 'King' working ceased in September 1962, and all 30 members of the class were withdrawn during that year. Sadly, *King Henry III* was photographed for the last time, being cut up in 'C' Shop at Swindon.

26th April 1964

Sic transit gloria mundi.